STUART McHARDY is a storyteller, writer, poet, musician, broadcaster and lecturer on Scottish history and folklore. Since graduating with a history degree from Edinburgh University in the 1970s he has found ongoing inspiration and stimulus in Scotland's dynamic story and music traditions. His research has led him far beyond his native land and he has lectured and performed in many different parts of the world. Whether telling stories to children or lecturing to adults, Stuart's enthusiasm and love of his material make him an entertaining and stimulating speaker.

His own enthusiasm and commitment have led to him re-interpreting much of the history, mythology and legends of early Western Europe. Combining the roles of scholar and performer gives McHardy an unusually clear insight into tradition and he sees connections and continuities that others may have missed. As happy singing an old ballad as analysing ancient legends, he has held such diverse positions as Director of the Scots Language Resource Centre and President of the Pictish Arts Society. He lives in Edinburgh with the lovely Sandra and they have one son, Roderick.

D0911690

By the same author

Strange Secrets of Ancient Scotland (Lang Syne Publishers, 1989)

Tales of Whisky and Smuggling (Lochar, 1992)

The Wild Haggis an the Greetin-faced Nyaff (Scottish Children's Press, 1995)

Scotland: Myth, Legend and Folklore (Luath Press, 1999)

Edinburgh and Leith Pub Guide (Luath Press, 2000)

Scots Poems to be read aloud (Editor) (Luath Press, 2001)

Tales of Whisky and Smuggling (House of Lochar, 2002)

The Quest for Arthur (Luath, 2002)

The Quest for the Nine Maidens (Luath Press, 2003)

MacPherson's Rant and other tales of the Scottish Fiddle (Birlinn, 2004)

The Silver Chanter and other tales of Scottish Piping (Birlinn, 2004)

School of the Moon: the Scottish cattle raiding tradition (Birlinn, 2004)

On the Trail of Scotland's Myths and Legends (Luath Press, 2005)

The Well of the Heads and other Clan Tales (Birlinn, 2005)

Luath Storyteller: Tales of the Picts (Luath, 2005)

On the Trail of the Holy Grail (Luath, 2006)

The White Cockade and other Jacobite Tales (Birlinn, 2006)

Luath Storyteller: Tales of Edinburgh Castle (Luath, 2007)

Luath Storyteller Series
Tales of Whisky

STUART McHARDY

Luath Press Limited

EDINBURGH

www.luath.co.uk

First published 2010

ISBN 978-1-906817-41-1

The paper used in this book is neutral sized and
recyclable. It is made from elemental chlorine free
pulps sourced from renewable forests.

Printed and bound by
CPI Bookmarque, Croydon CRO 4TD

Typeset in 10.5 point Sabon by
3btype.com

contents

OUR NATIONAL BEVERAGE

HISKY IS JUST ABOUT the world's favourite drink. And quite right too. It comes in many shapes and forms and some of our cousins (the Irish and the Americans) like to claim that they too manufacture the *cratur*, the amber nectar, the wasp, the nippy sweetie; other countries even on the other side of our planet now claim to make their own. However, everybody knows there is only one real true whisky – Scotch.

There are many kinds of Scotch and the variety of single malts – which are the best of the finest – continues to rise exponentially, all marketed in ever more creative ways. Nowadays, it would hardly be a surprise to find a Highland malt matured for 50 years in a pair of Sir Walter Scott's old *breeks*. No doubt some aficionados could talk for hours on the nose of that. The truth is of course that whisky was invented for a single, practical reason – to offset Scotland's weather. Some say it was to counteract that uniquely Scottish institution – the *dreich* day, when the traditional combination of cold wet and biting wind sets the teeth to chattering, the fingers to shaking and the soul to cry out for solace and help. The unfortunate truth is that it was not created to counteract the *dreich* day but the *dreich* week and possibly even the *dreich* month, which is of course a traditional Scottish term for July in alternate years.

Before rapacious governments turned whisky into a tax raising bonanza, forcing its manufacture into the hands of industrialists, people made their own; you may be lucky enough to meet one or two who still do so, working at their still in the hills. Known as peatreek, from all accounts it was superb stuff. It was generally left to mature for at least three days and the best of the sublime throat-slacker, four times distilled, was so strong it was never served to children under three years old.

There is that well known story by Mrs Elizabeth Grant of Ardvorlich visiting a logging camp near the headwaters of the Spey in the early 19th century. It was hard, often cold work and at the mid-morning break it was customary for the men to line up to get a nip of whisky. Mrs Grant was shocked to see a woman and wee lad of about eight years old lining up with the men for a dram. When both the woman and then the boy took the whisky she felt she had to say something to the laddie.

'Do you always take a dram of whisky when offered?'

'Och, that I do missus,' the lad replied.

'But, that is whisky,' she said. 'Doesn't it bite?'

'Och aye,' he said, 'but I fair like the bite!'

It's one of those things that are all too easily forgotten but Temperance movements, exhortations to 'sensible drinking' and other attempts at social control are a result of the industrialisation and profiteering of alcohol, not its creation.

Nowadays the once secret process, carried on in smoke filled bothies in the hills (and city back street tenements), is undertaken in clean and sparkly distilleries the length and breadth of the country. Many of these allow visitors to tour their premises with a guide and some of these are even free. What never fails to puzzle many of the indigenous population is how people can tour so many different distilleries – most of which are effectively much the same as each other – but then we remember there are trainspotters and stamp collectors. However, as the study of whisky necessitates a wee sample perhaps the comparison is overstated. We do have to say that meeting a certain Japanese gentlemen a few years back gave us great cause for concern. His home in Yokohama was lined with glass fronted cases all full of bottles of whisky, hundreds of them – and all unopened! To the true Scot this is sacrilege. You are under no obligation to throw away the cork once it is out of the neck of the whisky bottle, but that is how we were raised! We do however believe in using glasses, drinking whisky straight from the bottle is uncouth – it might lead to spillage. Some of the stories in this wee volume have been handed down in the McDrouthy family who are distant relations, but happy to share their family traditions with a wider audience.

As to how you take your whisky, that is up to you, but the original McDrouthy put it simply: the only things that should go into a dram of whisky is a wee drop of water, or another dram.

A selection of toasts

Slainte, (Slancha)
Gaelic for 'Your Good Health'

Up yer Kilt
An invitation to jollity to members of either sex

Lang may yer lum reek and yer wallie dreep
A wish for future prosperity

Mair
A Scots term that translates directly into several
languages. 'More beer or wine etc.

Some Scottish drinking terms

Merry
having ingested sufficient drink to believe all is
well with the world – often in spite of immediate
reality.

Fleein
in a state of joy through drink.

Guttered
a bit more than *fleein*.

Stotious
somewhere in between *fleein* and *guttered*.

Banjaxed
inebriated to the point of imminent sleep.

Oot o it
past the point of being *banjaxed* and in the arms
of Morpheus (asleep, or perhaps comatose is
closer)

Etiquette

It is wise to be aware of some of the rules of
drinking in Scotland. Because we traditionally
drink in rounds, once you have accepted a drink
in company it is expected you will 'stand your
hand' and buy the company a drink. All others
in the company are obliged to follow suit, so be
warned. There are those who abuse this and as
such are generally frowned upon and
unwelcome.

In busy *howffs* it is sometimes difficult to
attract the attention of busy bar staff when it's
your turn to buy a round comes, but be patient
and please do not yell or whistle – holding up
a large denomination note will usually suffice.

BLADDERED

I'S AN INTERESTING WORD – *bladdered*. Nowadays, it is generally used as a descriptive term meaning that the subject has indulged in slightly more drink than is good for one, is perhaps a little bit under the weather or more generally knee-walking, wall-banging, short-sighted, brain-dead drunk. In these days of political correctness and the government consistently acting like a frigid old spinster with a ferret in her drawers, we are all supposed to be in favour of responsible drinking. Well, my pal the Man from Fife always described responsible drinking as remembering to restock the cupboard before the money ran out – and who I am I to gainsay a man of such intemperate appetite and wide experience. But back to bladdered – we all know what our bladder is, the repository for beer and spirits while the rest of our physiology extracts the benefit of the wondrous nectars to alter the way we perceive the world. It may have been Winston Churchill who, when accused of being drunk, replied, 'Ah yes madam, but I will be sober in the morning while you will still be ugly/stupid/

miserable/as tight as a duck's arse in a rainstorm.' Take your pick. However, in the long and illustrious history of self-induced brain damage in old Scotland, bladders had another aspect.

Back in the good old days of widespread illicit whisky distilling there was an effective war between the government and the peatreekers – the Scottish cottage industry whisky makers whose descendants became in time the moonshiners of Appalachia who struggled so gallantly against the stupidity of the Volstead Act in America and won the day. The peatreekers, who were active in many Scottish towns and cities as well as in the Highlands, were people who saw no reason why the government should tax what they made from the crops they or their friends and relatives, grew themselves. If it was God's bounty that they could make porridge from their oats why should there be any flaming limit on what they brewed and distilled from their barley? It was a matter of honour that such intrusions by the greedy tax-collecting gentlemen of the Excise had to be resisted at all costs. In the 18th and early 19th century there was an added advantage for the peatreekers. The spirits that were made in large distilleries – favoured by the government because they could so easily be taxed – were toe-curlingly, teeth-gratingly and mind-bendingly awful and people throughout the expanding cities of the industrial revolution much preferred the real stuff.

Of course, as we all know once government – and the pathetic, approval-seeking, self-centred, avaricious and ambitious scum who aspire to run governments a.k.a. politicians – get an idea in their heads it is hard to shift. So the peatreekers were persecuted the length and breadth of Scotland by those men of the Excise they knew as gaugers. And a scabrous, dirty-fingered bunch they generally were. People who couldn't spell 'honesty' if it bit them on the arse! Their job was to prevent the whisky manufactured in the hills and mountains of Scotland – just like today, the most preferred stuff due to the quality of Highland water – from getting to its thirsty markets in the cities.

In order to circumvent the inquisition of the gaugers many tricks were resorted to. One of the most common was the use of bladders. The bladder of a goat will hold enough for a good night for two or three people, that of a pig for quite a few more and the bladder of a cow, ox or bull held enough for a considerable number of smiling faces, happy songs and possibly even a bit of 'houghmagandie'*.

The advantage of the bladder, once fitted with a non-leaking stopper attachment was that it could be hidden in a whole series of places. That famous film *Whisky Galore* showed the initiative of Hebridean islanders in hiding bottles of whisky collected from the wreck of the ss *Politician*, but imagine how much more flexible bladders were. They could be hidden in pails of milk, in loads of hay, straw or vegetables, under babies in cots, and most helpfully of all, under articles of clothing. There were even examples in the 18th century of people having bladders under their hats! The hats concerned may have been 'tiles', as they were known, top hats which had plenty room for a goat's bladder at least. And of course bladders had the advantage of utilising an everyday object that was otherwise of limited use and was totally environmentally sustainable.

* the act of replicating the species through mating – though it is more fun than that sounds, honest.

the angels' share

OW, THE PHRASE the Angels' Share is well enough known to whisky drinkers. It is used to refer to the whisky that evaporates through the wood of the barrel in the long, slow maturing process that eventually creates that most supreme of human achievements, that nectar of the Gods, Scotch Whisky. It is generally reckoned that about two per cent of the good stuff is thus spirited away annually. This accounts for the horrendous prices charged for malt whisky over 15 years old. The angels' share is made up for by the increase in price. The idea that it is taken by angels is hardly surprising when we consider just how sublime and transcendent single malt whisky is, in fact it gives a totally different aspect to the meaning of spiritual. However this is not the only way spirit that has historically disappeared from within the confines of the bonded warehouses of Scotland.

Many years ago, when McDrouthy was still a young lad – which, despite rumours to the contrary, was long after the *Titanic* had set sail and sunk – there were certain bargains to be had in some of Scotland's major cities. McDrouthy had the privilege of being a student – a form of life that has been compared to a parasitic growth on all forms of alcohol (a tradition that McDrouthy the Younger has carried on splendidly) – in the capital. Here he came across rumours of that Scottish Holy Grail, cheap whisky! Now it ill behoves people from other lands to cast nasturtiums at the Scot's traditional thrift, for by 'cheap' here, we are not referring to either the ingredients or the methodology of production of the amber nectar, merely the price. It was also whisky that was available through that most Scottish of virtues – enterprise! For it seems that towards the end of autumn in a local bonded warehouse an accident would invariably occur to a certain whisky that must remain nameless, though the colour of the bottle was significant. This was the dropping of a full vat of whisky in such a peculiar place that the entire contents of the barrel disappeared through the drains. It was also extremely strange that this happened when no members of the Excise were on duty at the bond, due to some kind of training meeting elsewhere.

This was of course a great tragedy, or it

might have been if not for the aforesaid enterprise. For as it happened this unforeseen accident always took place when several smaller barrels and other receptacles were, totally by chance, to hand. This meant that the endangered spirits could in fact be prevented from entering the drains and going forth to pollute the local river. Through manful efforts and absolute dedication almost all of the contents of the barrel were saved. However, the customs seal on the barrel was also broken in the process and there was no way to replace that. Therefore, it was considered expedient by all present that the 'gentlemen' of the Excise (and that is certainly not the only thing they have been called down the years) should be informed that the entire contents of the barrel had been lost.

This incident, which involved the entire community of employees in the warehouse, meant that there would be some extra Christmas spirit for one and all. It was McDrouthy's great fortune to be acquainted with the brother of one of the employees, and thus able to purchase a bottle of the good stuff at a knock-down price. For some unknown reason – and this has been investigated by many a dedicated scientist –

whisky on which no duty has been paid to the government always tastes better. At the time however, it had not crossed the young McDrouthy's mind – he was after all merely a stripling – how the said beverage had been spirited out of the Bonded Warehouse, which like all the others was under the constant watchful eye of the Her Majesty's Customs and Excise.

In fact it was not until many years later that the truth of this mystery was revealed. During the presentation of a show about Scottish drinking at one Edinburgh Festival Fringe in the early years of this century, McDrouthy was holding forth on the use of animal bladders for transporting illicit whisky back in the 18th and 19th centuries. He mentioned that one favoured method was to have these bladders moved past the watchful gaugers (employees of the then Customs and Excise who were rarely, if ever, gentlemen by any reckoning) by hiding them under the nether garments of members of the gentler sex – a process that at the time was believed to induce a kind of secondary distillation due to the proximity of the amber nectar to the warmer parts of the female anatomy. Be that as it may, such whisky was

considered to be of the best. While expounding
in his usual pompous matter on this topic,
our hero mentioned that he had of course
as a student obtained some 'appropriated' spirit.

He was then interrupted by a member of the
audience who enquired as to the name of the
particular whisky. Now such interruptions can
call forth a range of reactions from performers.
Some carry cans of CS spray, others a library of
cutting remarks and yet others a pocket of curare
tipped darts with which to see off the scabrous
bastard who has dared to interrupt the
performance. However in this instance the
contribution was welcome.

On being told the name of the whisky –
which must remain secret to protect the guilty –
the man in the audience then said, 'Well, you
might be interested in knowing how the spilled
whisky was smuggled out of the bond.'

'I am sure we all would be,' said McDrouthy,
and both other members of the audience
concurred.

'Well, it was taken out in bottles tucked
into the stocking tops of the young lasses who
worked in the office,' said his informant.

'Wait a minute,' McDrouthy replied,'

I remember the time well and that young ladies were generally clad in mini-skirts, some of which were little more than pelmets.'

'Ah yes,' he said with a smile, 'but an aspirin bottle of whisky could be hidden safely even under a mini-skirt. And it doesn't take more than a week or two to fill a bottle that way...'

Now the thought of all that whisky, smuggled out nestling against the soft flesh of a young lady's inner thigh, is quite enough to make me reach for that 25 year old Highland Whisky I keep for special occasions... and if memory serves that whisky did taste particularly fine.

What it goes to show is that good ideas never die.

atholl brose

GIVEN THE SUBLIME nature of whisky it is little wonder that over the years it has been used as a flavouring for a range of delicacies and as a main ingredient of others. Although the life of the average Scots a few hundred years ago may have been a bit coarse by today's standards, if you made your own whisky, or had a ready access to it, a plentiful supply would generally be to hand and there would be no need to be overly precious about using it in a variety of ways. One of the better known whisky recipes is of course Atholl Brose and here is one particular recipe.

Ingredients
3 rounded tablespoons of medium oatmeal
2 tablespoons heather honey
Scotch whisky

Method
The oatmeal is prepared by putting it into a basin and mixing it with cold water until the consistency is that of a thick paste. Leave for half an hour and then put through a fine strainer,

pressing with a wooden spoon to extract as much liquid as possible. Throw away the oatmeal and use the creamy liquor from the oatmeal for the brose.

Mix four dessert spoonfuls of pure honey and four sherry glassfuls of the prepared oatmeal and stir well. (Purists insist on a silver spoon for stirring!) Put into a quart bottle and fill with malt whisky. Shake before serving.

Now it should be said that there is absolutely no need to have access to a silver spoon. This is a drink to be drunk in all kinds of houses. However it being a Scottish drink there is of course a story as to its origin...

Long, long ago in Atholl, nowadays the upper parts of the Perthshire, there was a giant. Now, giants were relatively common back in the day, but this one was a real pest. He had nothing but contempt for humans and saw nothing wrong with preying upon such puny creatures. So he would help himself to anybody's cattle, anytime he wished. He was also likely to turn up and gather an entire grain store into his enormous sack. As everybody had to grow enough food to feed themselves in those

days, it was no wonder that many brave men
and women tried their best to stop the giant
stealing their precious stores and cattle.
As a result many died, and often enough the
giant ended up wiping out entire communities.
Often they would not be found for some time;
there were far too many instances of somebody
coming to visit an isolated Highland clachan
only to find the mangled bodies of its inhabitants
strewn around and the grain store burst open
and empty. Others simply ended up starving
to death or barely surviving through the help
of neighbouring clachans, who themselves lived
close to the edge of self-sufficiency.

The giant was a terrible blight on the country
and a wild and vicious creature to the core,
but strangely enough he had a daughter.
She was more like a tall human than an
actual giant and she was exceedingly beautiful,
with long black hair, flashing brown eyes,
a curvaceous figure and a brilliant smile.
Of her mother there was no sign. Her life was
pretty lonely and although the giant loved her,
she longed for company of people her own age;
truth to tell she would have liked any company
at all. The only others she ever met were the

occasional visiting giants, most of whom were,
like her father, boorish, ill-tempered and very
smelly. Though coming from giant parents,
she was in all ways much more like a human
and her heart hoped one day that she might
be lucky enough to find herself a husband.
But how? No human would come near her.
Or so she thought.

Due to the giant's depredations, the bens
and glens around the beautiful wee valley where
he and the lass lived were empty of humans.
Only the occasional brave soul would venture
into the area, chasing stray cattle or goats,
and very, very occasionally some brave young
lad would come up to the high mountain passes
to hunt deer. So it was that a young lad called
Dougal was out hunting in the hills one day.
He knew he was near to where the giant had
his dwelling and he had half a mind to see if he
could locate it. He could then return with a large
force of men and ambush the ogre; if they caught
him by surprise they could maybe put an end to
him and all the trouble he caused. So it was that
he came out of the woods on the hill above the
giant's great crumpled heap of a home. From
a distance it just looked like a vast heap of rocks.

If there wasn't smoke coming from the hearth inside he wouldn't have given it a second glance. However, as Dougal looked down into the wee glen he saw movement. Thinking it might be a fine stag, he threw himself to the ground and, slowly raising his head, peered down.

There between the great jumbled rock mass and the fine sparkling burn that ran about 30 yards from it, he saw a young woman. And what a woman! With the keen eye of one raised to the hunt, he clearly saw not just a female but a young female and more than that, an absolute beauty. Then as the wind shifted he heard her singing. It was a sad, almost keening song that rose up on the air and the voice itself was glorious. He was transfixed as the lass went to the stream, filled the bucket she was carrying and returned to what he now realised must be the giant's dwelling. He had just decided to brave things out by going to the house and speaking to the lass when he heard a great roar. Lying perfectly still he slowly turned his head and looked down the glen. There, striding up the path was the giant, his great sack bulging over his shoulder. As he watched the lass came out and her

father showed her the contents of his pack.
There were cattle, goats, chickens and geese,
and bags and bags of oats and barley, enough
to keep several clachans going for the winter.
Dougal's heart was no longer filled with longing
for the lass but hatred for this vile creature
who was continually wreaking havoc amongst
the people of Atholl. Once the giant had
bundled up his booty back into the sack
and gone into his house with the lass,
Dougal rose up and headed home, his head
filled with thoughts of how he could rid the
world of this giant. True he had fallen for
his daughter, but the need to rid Atholl of
this curse was his main desire.

Over the coming weeks his family and
friends noticed that he had gone quiet. Most
of them thought he had fallen for some lass
but they had no idea what was going on.
He thought again of ambush but realised
that such a plan might bring the giant's daughter
into danger too. He knew fine that he didn't
want her harmed; he wanted to make her his
own. Courtship though was not an option.
He would just have to get rid of her father first
then trust to fortune that he could make the

lass accept him. But how was he to get rid
of the giant? Then he remembered. On one
of the well-worn paths near to the giant's
home he had come across a great stone that
was hollowed out. It was twice the size of the
biggest iron cauldron he had ever seen and
he had wondered if this was some sort of cup
that the giant might use. There was one way
to find out. He had a plan.

Now, although he was young, he was a lad
of some intelligence and like many Highlanders
was both fond of whisky and had a bit of
a sweet tooth. He was prepared to take a
bet that the giant was much the same. So,
for three nights he made the journey to the
great stone. On the first night he carried two
ankers or small barrels of whisky; on the
second night, a great sack of the finest ground
oatmeal, and on the third night he took up
another anker of whisky and a great earthenware
pot full of the finest heather honey. This time
he wrapped himself up in his plaid and lay
down to sleep among some nearby trees.

In the morning after his third trip he was
up at dawn and poured the ingredients into the
hollow in the stone. Using one of the now empty

whisky barrels, he brought water from a nearby
stream. Then, using a thick branch cut from
a tree, he stirred the ingredients till they began
to froth and just as the heady aroma of the
brew began to fill his nostrils, he heard a noise.
It was the giant coming through the woods from
his house. Dougal barely had time to throw
the barrels, sack and pot into the bushes and
dive in after before the giant came into sight.
Coming down the path the giant walked
towards the hollow stone. Just as it looked
as if he was going to stride right past, he
stopped, crinkled his nose and took a deep
breath. He let out a great 'Hmmm,' and turned
to look around. Spotting the great cauldron-like
boulder he bent over it and sniffed again.
This time the sound that erupted was a mighty
'Aha!' which caused all the birds within at
least a hundred yards to take off in fright.
The giant leant down and took a sip of the
frothing brew.

He let out a great whoop and, picking up
the great, grey stone, he began to drink the
delectable mixture down. He kept on drinking
till he emptied the vessel. Then he wiped
his hand over his mouth, gave a great belch,

a wild laugh, and throwing the boulder
to one side, headed off down the glen.
At once he began to sing. Well, that's what
Dougal thought it was. In truth it was a horrible,
growling noise, like boulders clashing in a
tumbling burn, but the way the giant was soon
waving his hands about, Dougal reckoned he
was feeling happy. And so he should he had
three barrels of whisky inside him! The giant
began to stride even faster and Dougal soon
had to run to keep him in sight.

As the giant came further and further down
the mountain, Dougal began to have doubts.
He had no idea how much whisky a giant
could take. What if it just made him even
wilder than usual? He hadn't thought about
that. Just as he began to get frightened by
what he had done, he noticed that the giant
had slowed down. As he hid behind a tree he
noticed a wee stagger, then another. Soon the
giant had slowed right down and was knocking
over trees as he bumped into them. Dougal's
plan appeared to be working! Within a couple
of minutes the giant tripped and fell. He pulled
himself up into a sitting position with his back
against a great oak tree and within a minute

or two was fast asleep. His snore rang out like thunder through the forest.

Now, Dougal had his chance. With the thundering noise ringing in his ears, he was sure the great creature was deep into a drink-induced sleep. Drawing his sword he came down the path. Without hesitation he came up beside the giant and drove his sword right through the beast's great hairy ear and into his brain. The giant never felt a thing as the life left his body and the great thundering snores fell silent. Dougal had done it. He had got rid of the Giant of Atholl. He knew he would be a hero to all the people of Atholl, but what would giant's daughter think?

He headed straight back up the mountain to find out. When he told her what he had done she realised that her old life was gone for ever. And Morag, for that was her name, realised that this young man had opened up a whole new life for her. Although she had been brought up by a great, uncouth giant, she was a woman first and could see in Dougal's eyes that he was deeply in love with her. So, she consented to leave her high mountain home and head down into Atholl with the young man. Dougal was of course considered a great hero when people heard of his exploit and they thought it all the better that when they told the story of how he had conquered the giant, to give this story its real true flavour, they had to serve Atholl Brose along with the telling. It soon became a popular story indeed!

the Buchan twa bunnet trick

OW, THERE ARE THOSE who will tell you that the reason that whisky was invented was the Scottish weather and they may just have a point. I have friends from the north of Sweden, just outside the Arctic Circle, who occasionally come over for the *craic*. They are used to several feet of snow lasting for months every winter and one local sport in Umea, where some of them work, is to bet which date in spring the frozen boats in the river will be able to move. Their public buildings are all very well insulated and of course they have very efficient clothing. However when they come to Scotland they have problems. This is because while they are used to snow, and possibly even a bit of rain or sleet, all these varying types of precipitation tend to fall vertically in Sweden. In Scotland, due to the unceasing winds, rain is usually of the horizontal type, and it is the same with hail, sleet and snow. However, due to our peculiar geographical location – Edinburgh is after all as far north as Moscow – in winter we sometimes tend to get all these forms of precipitation

together. Thus you can have a day that starts off sunny, then the grey clouds grumble in and suddenly we are hit with filthy squalls of combined precipitation driven by fierce winds that cut like a knife! It is little wonder then that my Swedish friends find our weather inclement. We have a specific word for the weather when it combines the aspects of extreme wet, bone-shivering cold and ear-blistering wind – *dreich*. It is a word that sums up the feeling that this weather induces and it is likely that it was to offset the *dreichness* that whisky was created all those years ago. Culture being what it is in Scotland, there are perhaps remnants of belief from such ancient times.

One of these, passed on to me by a good friend, the Buchan Loon, is the 'Buchan twa bunnet trick'. This piece of ancient folklore has come down through generations of his family, none of whom, he is keen to stress, were ever Rechabites, tea-totallers or other variations on the sad souls who see sobriety as the ultimate goal of mankind. This piece of long nurtured folk-wisdom is an example of the fact that many old forms of knowledge are always worth considering precisely because they have survived. Here is the good word.

On being struck down with the lurgie, the flu,

the sniffles, or any other of the 73½ variants of
the cold that Scotland can throw at you, the
procedure is as follows. Take to your bed.
Place your bunnet, bonnet, hat or titfer on the
bed post (if you don't have a bed post anywhere
in plain sight will suffice) Then instruct your
significant other, or wife if you have one, to
bring you a hot toddy – one recipe is given below
– and drink it while it is still hot. As soon as it is
finished repeat the process. Keep doing this until
you can see twa bunnets. At which point put
your head on the pillow and close your eyes.
You will immediately be overcome with an all-
enveloping sense of cosiness and happiness that
will transport you off to the Land of Nod.
When you awaken in the morning you will be
better. If not, repeat till the desired effect is attained.

In the event of living on one's own as a result
of employing the Buchan twa-bunnet trick too
often, something of the same effect can be
attained by plugging a kettle into a socket near
the bed and making the toddies yourself – but
this is not as much fun. There *are* those however,
who will tell you in all seriousness that you are
better off with an electric kettle than a wife.
I have been instructed to tell you that you
should avoid such people.

a toddy recipe

Ingredients
Scotch Whisky of your choice – 50 ml (2 fl oz)
[at least]
Boiling water
Lemon juice – 1 tablespoon (optional)
Cube sugar (four pieces) or a tablespoon
of honey

Method
Half-fill a tumbler with hot water. When the
glass has reached a comfortable temperature,
pour it out and put ¾ pieces of cube sugar or the
honey in the glass. Pour in a wineglass of boiling
water and stir (silver spoons are recommended!).
When the sugar/honey is dissolved, add the
lemon juice then add the whisky and stir.
Sip with 'tender loving care'

early whisky

RGUMENTS HAVE RAGED for many years as to how long whisky has been made in Scotland. Nobody in their right mind – sober or otherwise – doubts that it was invented here, but when? Some people hold to the idea that Europeans in the early Middle Ages learned the art of distilling from Arabs who had originally got the trick from the Chinese. The problem is that the earliest whisky makers never bothered to write anything down. They were far too busy sampling their own wares to think about keeping records. There was no government trying to extort taxes from them and in all truth they were probably illiterate! A while back I was mulling over this question with a friend of mine, the noted Gaelic scholar Professor Ken MacKinnon. Ken has the privilege of living at Ferintosh on the Black Isle, the home of the first government licensed distillery and arguably the location for the birth of Scotland's most important industry. I mentioned to him that I had been reading the works of Taliesin, the early Welsh poet, and had come across an interesting snippet in a poem entitled *The Hostile Conspiracy*. This said, 'I have been a grain discovered on a hill. The Harvester took me to free my essence in a place full of smoke.'

This had intrigued me and I had asked a professor of Celtic what he thought it meant. He had said that it probably was a reference to the drying of hallucinogenic mushrooms! We know that the ancient bards were prone to that kind of thing but I reckon the professor was wrong. Having been around and about in the '60s and '70s, I have had the pleasure of experimenting with such natural substances. Ain't it funny how so many people admit to having 'experimented' with drugs but never admit to having fun! However, if you tried to smoke-dry mushrooms you would end up with something utterly horrible and completely unpalatable – the proper way is to air dry them, but in the interests of keeping on the right side of the law I am not going to tell you more. I did however have an ulterior motive in asking. The concept of releasing the essence of grain in a place full of smoke is a precise description of how whisky was distilled in bothies – small huts – throughout the Highlands right up to the

19th century. The distillation was fired by peat and the bothies were so full of smoke that the illicit whisky makers were known as peatreekers – they smelt of the stuff all the time and could also be recognised by their blackened faces!

Now, Taliesin is thought to have been around possibly as early as the sixth century – *But,* I hear you thinking, *he was Welsh*. Maybe he was, but the ancestor of the Welsh language was spoken by many of our ancient tribal peoples including the Picts who occupied most of Scotland outside of Argyll, and from whom the McDrouthys have long claimed descent. In the Lowland areas, the Gododdin of Lothian and the Britons of Strathclyde all spoke early forms of Welsh too; so Taliesin, even if he didn't live in Scotland – and there are stories that he did – was part of a culture that stretched from Cornwall to the Far North. This is not to say that the Welsh should be considered as descendants of the Picts – unless they want to be – though the mutual conviviality between the Scots and Welsh is something to be treasured.

There was an ancient tale amongst the Picts that one of their chiefs had his son killed rather than give up the secret of making Heather Ale to his enemies. Some versions tell us the enemies were Scots from Argyll, and others that they were Romans, a rather boisterous and aggressive lot who were brief visitors north of Hadrian's Wall. Now I may be a bit thick but I can't see anybody defending the secret of brewing any type of beer to that extent. Whisky though is another matter.

I was wittering on about this, with glass in hand, to Professor MacKinnon and he said, 'You may have a point.' He had not long translated, from the Latin, The *Noli Pater*, a poem written by St Columba who also lived in the sixth century. In this, the good saint used a particular word – *siccera* – which has the specific meaning of strong drink and is never used of such watery stuff as beer, wine or mead. So, could the Early British peoples have been making whisky back in the First Millennium?

We know they had the technological skills necessary. The workmanship of the Deskford Carnyx, a first century war-trumpet found in Moray, shows they could make pretty good tubing. There was certainly plenty water, barley and peat. And we know that the Ancient Egyptians knew about distillation. Archaeologists tell us that 5,000 years ago people were sailing up and down the eastern shores of the Atlantic from Scandinavia to Morocco and into the Mediterranean – so it is quite possible that contacts were made over considerable distances.

Without getting distracted into complex linguistics – though I have been known to talk in tongues after a second bottle of the good stuff – it seems that whisky could well have been known amongst the different Celtic-speaking peoples of Early Britain. Those amongst you of a critical cast of mind may think that the argument suggests that it was maybe the Welsh that had the secret. Well, if they had have known about the creation of the elixir, they would have held on to it. It is not something anyone would forget! It is also an undeniable fact that the oldest known Welsh poem – called *The Gododdin* – was written at the dawn of the seventh century in Edinburgh! So I am suggesting that the bold Taliesin knew about it either from a visit to Scotland or one of his northern cousins bringing him a drop of the good stuff. Columba, of course, would have been very grateful for whisky to counteract the perennially rainy climate of the West of Scotland. So when next you raise your glass, have a toast to the ancient British tribesmen who may just have invented the finest drink ever known to man, or woman-kind.

the picts and drink

OR MOST OF our time on this planet, human beings lacked the art of writing. Knowledge of all kinds, history, genealogy, mythology and what we now think of as science could only be passed on by example or through word of mouth – storytelling. Storytelling is not a precise science and, unlike history, is rarely concerned with specific dates, times or even whether people in the story ever actually existed. Still, though we can learn a lot from stories, we do have to be prepared to take a critical view – something that can certainly be enhanced by having a drop of the good stuff to help you think! There is that old Scottish story of the Heather Yill, which has been preserved in the McDrouthy family – some of whom are themselves so well preserved they are permanently pickled. The version in the McDrouthy tradition differs in that it tells us that Yill was not in fact heather ale, but whisky. You can make up your own mind as to whether a tale of this particular charm could ever really have occurred regarding something as simple as ale, universally known and drunk throughout the world at some time or another, or whether it must have been about something much more complicated and mysterious to create.

Amongst their contemporaries – the Scots, Britons and in later years the Norsemen – the Picts were particularly envied for one thing. It wasn't their great strength or their remarkable stamina, though both made them fearsome enemies. What the other peoples wanted for themselves was the recipe for Heather Yill, the strong sweet alcoholic drink that the Picts, well versed in ancient herbal lore, made from the tops of the heather plant. Given the amount of heather that grows in Scotland, the advantages of being able to make drink from it were obvious. Heather was something no one would ever run out of! However the Picts, though happy enough to trade their yill for other goods – and usually exacting a high price – were absolutely firm in their refusal to hand over the recipe. The leader or chief of each community or tribe of the Picts was the one who had the knowledge and this was passed from father to son. Sons were always given the secret so if the father fell in battle someone would be able to carry on the tradition.

One time a chief of one of the Scottish tribes went on a raid to Galloway with the specific idea of getting the secret, and he kidnapped a number of Pictish warriors. All of them were tortured extensively but not one of them would say a word about the Heather Yill. The Scots didn't know that only the chiefs and their sons had the knowledge and all of the Pictish warriors went to their deaths before giving up even that secret!

The frustration of the Scots increased but one day they had the good fortune – they thought – to come upon the chief of the Picts and his son near a cliff-top on the Rhinns of Galloway. There was no escape. Behind the elderly Pict and his son there was only the sea and before them 20 odd heavily armed Scots warriors.

'Surrender or die,' called the leader of the Scots and the old Pict put down his spear, followed by his son.

'Now,' said the Scottish chief, 'we want to know the secret of the Heather Yill. If you

don't tell us we will kill you both, and we'll
take our time in doing it!'

'Well,' said the Pictish chief, 'before I tell
ye, ye'll have to do something for me.'

'And what's that?' asked the Scots
suspiciously.

'Well, ye see it would shame me to give
away the secrets of my ancestors in front
of my son here. So ye'll have to kill him.'

'WHAT?' gasped the Scot as the young
Pict looked at his father with terror in his eyes,
his mouth open in disbelief.

'Aye, aye. That's the way it has to be,'
said the old grey-haired Pict, slowly shaking
his head and looking sadly at his son.

The Scottish chief took him at his word
and before the young Pict had really understood
what was happening, he was lying dead at his
father's feet.

'Now then,' said the Scot, 'what about it?'

'What about what?' answered the Pict.

'This Heather Yill, the recipe, that's
what,' rasped the Scot. 'You said you'd
tell us once your son was dead. He's lying
there like a log at your feet. Now give us
the recipe.'

'Och aye,' said the Pict slowly. 'So I did. And you believed me?'

'Aye, we believed you,' replied the Scot. 'That's why we killed your laddie.'

'Ach well' said the Pict with a wee smile. 'Ye might as well kill me too, for I'll never tell you how to brew the heather Yill.'

And so they did.

fechtin whisky

HE MAKING OF illicit whisky could be a profitable business and some families did very well out of it. One such family invested some of their profits in a tavern in a seaside Fife town which became known far and wide for the quality of the *uisge beatha* on sale. It was run by one of the sons called Jock. Jock had been set up in the business by the family due to the fact that he had been born with a deformed left leg which necessitated him going around with a crutch tucked under his left oxter. This of course pretty much precluded him from taking part in the general business of the family, making and distributing the very finest hand-crafted nectar or illicit hooch. Because of the intransigent and aggressive attitudes of the government of the time this traditional cottage industry had generally to be conducted in out of the way places which were difficult to get to and there was also the occasional need to be ready to be 'on one's toes', or skedaddle at speed. Jock clearly could not be a part of the family firm's day-to-day business. So a pub was purchased and Jock prove himself a fine publican indeed, his physical infirmity in no way diminishing his charm, conviviality and wit. Unusually for the time – and we are back in the early 19th century here, long before the advent of the horseless carriage (automobile), the wireless (radio) and other even more technologically advanced gizmos created to occupy one's time and distract oneself from everyday life – McDrouthy's was famous for the variety of different whiskies on offer, several of which were of course sourced from his brothers, cousins and even more far flung relatives. Back then the principal occupation of the adult population outside of work was of course the conviviality of shared experience that we nowadays know as going to the pub and McDrouthy's did a roaring trade.

The host was a jovial character, who would of course sip the occasional small glass himself and was known for always being ready for a laugh. He used to joke with his regulars that the range of whiskies he supplied were created to a specific set of requirements. Some of it was best for singing, another type for playing games (dominoes and draughts were popular

at the time) and others for philosophical
discussion or even the ancient Scottish art
of flyting. This bardic art came from the far
past in Scotland's Celtic and Norse culture
and was a formalized competition of insult.
While in the past participation was restricted
to poets who would draw upon deep-seated
vocabularies of invective to insult their fellow
poets in public, by this time it was slightly
debased and could often descend into little
more than streams of curses being exchanged
between friends – a milder form has survived
in many places even today. It was this particular
activity that led to one wag, asking Jock,
'How many curses in that cask then?'
Some topics for discussion were frowned on,
such as religion and politics, apart from the
general, if not universal, condemnation of
government in all shapes and sizes, particularly
in regard to the iniquitous taxation of drink.

One Saturday afternoon, Jock's tavern filled
up with a sudden influx of men. Some of them
were navvies from the nearby railway track that
was being laid while another group were sailors
from a man-o-war that was anchored at Rosyth.
Many of both groups were men in their 20s,

and like young men everywhere, not exactly
calm and collected. The inherent stupidity
of young men is always increased by numbers;
a couple of lads together are fine but once
you have half a dozen or more there is
a momentum towards boorishness, idiocy
and anti-social behaviour. Throw in another
group of similar numbers close by and the
scene is set for all sorts of non-intellectual
activity.

So it was, that fine day in Dunfermline;
the navvies and the sailors started off just
looking at each other, then glowering, then
sniping verbally. That long beloved phrase
of the Nobel-prize winners of the planet,
'What are you looking at, pal?' was soon
followed by, 'Think ye're somebody, do ye?'
and other bon mots. By this point several
individuals on either side were on their feet
and the posturing began to take on a heavier
note. Soon there was a bit of shoving and it
became clear to one and all that things were
about to take a turn for the worst.It was at
that point that Jock intervened.

'Gentlemen, gentlemen,' he shouted as he
hirpled his way in to the centre of the pub

where the confrontation was heating up.
'Gentlemen I have to beg your pardon there
has been a terrible mix-up. Please forgive me.'

All eyes focused on the crippled publican
who stood there in the midst of the brewing
storm, his bunnet in his hands and wearing
what could be described as a hang-dog look.
The room was silent as he stood there. Then,
with a deep sigh, he continued.

'Ach I must be gettin soft in the head boys.
I have been servin you all the wrong kind of
whisky.'

This caused total confusion in his audience
who began looking at each other with puzzled
looks. The wrong kind of whisky? Whatever
could he mean?

'Aye, aye the barrels got mixed up lads and
for the last half hour we have been serving you
all the fechtin whisky. Just pass your glasses back
to the bar and they'll be replaced with stuff from
the new barrel – the finest singin whisky
I have ever managed to find in my life. And the
next two drams are on the house!'

By the time those two free drams had
been drunk, there was indeed singing from
the navvies and the navy boys who were mixed

up across the pub and acting as if they had
all been lifelong friends.

In later years, some of Jock's customers
would remind him of this day and he would
tell them there were more types of whisky
than the singing and the fighting kinds,
but that some of them were not for discussion
in civilized company!

commitment

OW IT WAS LONG a matter of honour
for lairds – landowners, some of
whom were descended from chiefs
who had previously held the land
on behalf of their entire clan –
to be known as hospitable. In 17th and 18th
century Scotland this meant they would be
generous with drink and always have a good
supply to hand. In some cases this was claret,
Scotland's long friendship with France being
sealed with many a glass of wine, but in
many cases it was the 'wine of the country',
the golden treasure of the barley bree.

One such laird was old Meldrum of
Burnside. Like most of his compatriots who
owned land he was known by the name of his
house, Burnside. In truth he owned many other
farms but Burnside was a substantial stone-built
house at the centre of his estate and it was well
known for the jollity that occurred there on
a regular basis. Burnside was known as an
'auld farrant' or old-fashioned man. He liked
to stick to the old ways and in terms of
conviviality this had a certain meaning.

In the days when judges would happily
be quaffing claret during trials even in
the High Court and no tradesman's deal
was closed without a drink to seal it, Burnside
stuck to the traditional Scottish form of
hospitality. This meant whenever he invited
his friends for dinner, (which generally involved
combinations of prime beef, fresh salmon,
venison and game birds) they would drink
until they literally fell down or more likely
couldn't rise from their chairs. At this point
they would be carried to bed by Burnside's
servants, many of whom were fit young
ploughmen drafted in for the night and in
line for a good few drams themselves at a
later date.

Burnside himself was known to take the
lead in this conviviality but due to his constant
training was never amongst the first to fall.
He was, as they still say, a mannie that could
hold his drink, and his drink was whisky.
While he would have on hand plenty of claret
and even effete foreign imports like brandy
or gin, his tipple was the *uisge beatha*, the drink
of his fathers and despite his position as a local
magistrate, much of the amber fluid on offer at

his home had come from wee stills up a glen in the hills to the north of the house.

By the time of this one particular evening's entertainment, Burnside was well into his 60s. His first wife was long dead, his son and daughters living in Edinburgh and the second Mrs Burnside and her three children had gone off to live with a distant cousin in London, as far away as she could get from her husband and his bacchanalian ways. He wasn't that much bothered. He had his friends, his drink and if he wanted female company... he *was* the laird of Burnside wasn't he and there were quite a few handsome widows in the county.

Anyway, he had invited a group of his friends to stay for a day or two to partake of the old conviviality. As ever the food was grand, the drink flowing like water and everyone was having a good time. The first night went as it usually did with Burnside downing a couple of bottles of whisky all on his own before being dragged off to bed in the middle of the night. The second day, given the hangovers, the drinking started early and by eight o'clock the entire company were roaring *fou*. Everybody was having an absolutely grand time when one of the host's oldest pals, a Dundee lawyer called McNeil, noticed that Burnside was not in his chair.

'Where is mine host gone?' he asked the man next to him, Jamie Reid, another old friend who lived and farmed locally.

Reid was himself pretty far gone and pointed under the table.

McNeil clumsily lifted the table cloth and peered below. There stretched out his full length was Burnside, his face an unfortunate grey pallor.

'He's no looking well at all, man' said McNeil.

'Wheesht,' said Reid holding his finger to his lips. 'Dinnae say a word. He's stone dead and has been for the past twa or three hours. But he wouldnae want to spoil the party. Cheers.'

And they drank a toast to their late departed host who was true to the last.

whisky and religion

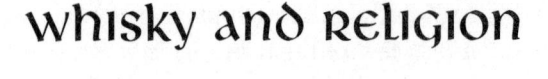OW WE HAVE HAD occasion to mention that there were those of a religious disposition who were against drink at various points in Scotland's history. The Temperance movement was at times very popular but there were those of a strong religious disposition who liked to drink. None more so than Big Archie, the postman who covered a widespread rural area. He was out in all weathers making sure that everybody got their mail and over the many years he had been in the job he had developed the habit of fortifying himself against the potential inclemency of the weather. Being a cheerful and generous soul he had become close friends with virtually everyone in the scattered community and several individuals, mainly small farmers who likewise had often to face the vagaries of our Scottish weather, liked the odd dram themselves. So it was, like many hard-working people throughout humanity, they would take a drink or two to set them up for their daily labour, and maybe the odd one or two to help them through the day

When Big Archie came by, it had become
the habit of a few of them to stop and have
a wee chat with the postman. Apart from the
good manners of politeness and interest, it was
a way of finding out what was happening in
the community. For Archie was always up to
date. Not that he was a gossip. No, he was
a concerned and responsible member of the
community who, because of his official position
nearly always knew what was developing.
And many of the local people only really
saw their neighbours at the kirk on Sunday,
the rest of the week being taken up in honest
toil. Those of us who live in modern cities
may not even know our neighbours but back
in the day in rural Scotland, people were aware
of the need for a sense of community to hold
them together and were always interested in
the goings on of their fellow citizens. Now most
of the community were more than happy to
chat with Archie on his route but these special
friends would offer him a dram to fortify
himself. And Archie was not a man to refuse.
He was also very much a Scot in his love of
discussion and debate, though not perhaps a
true example of that truly disputatious kind

of Scot who can start an argument on his own in a phone box.

Not only was Archie a deeply religious man with a prodigious memory for scripture and a well-developed skill in theological debate, he was an appreciator of nature. He saw all the creatures and the plants as evidence of God's work and this he explained was why he was often to be seen as the clock wore on towards noon, sitting in one or other of his favourite spots watching the glory of God's creation unfold around him. When asked why then did he sometimes have his eyes closed he would remind the enquirer that in order to truly appreciate the divine, it was necessary to meditate on the sublime ethereality of creation. This was what he would be doing if he had his eyes closed. He was an intelligent man and generally had an answer to any query of a theological or spiritual nature.

At this time, the latter years of the 19th century, the Temperance movement was gaining strength. So strong had it become that most of the congregation at the local kirk supported it and those who, like our hero, continued to drink were considered in need of help and guidance.

It wasn't so much the condemnation of
the righteous than the concern of the truly
charitable, for despite its bloody history, much
like of that of other religions, there have always
been many adherents of Christianity who were,
and are, essentially good-hearted folk.
Such people may seek to persuade but would
be very reluctant to dictate. And so it was
with our postie, he was the topic of many a
concerned chat, over cups of tea, and the odd
cake or two, amongst his neighbours and they
resolved to do something about helping him
with 'his wee problem'.

The first to try was the local doctor at whose
door Archie frequently called to deliver all sorts
of publications and pamphlets as well as regular
mail. One morning as the postie came to the
door the doctor invited him in. It was a late
September day and though the sun was shining
there was a snell edge to the wind that was
blowing and Archie happily accepted the offer
of a seat by the fire in the doctor's study for
a few minutes. So in they went and sat down.

After a few pleasantries about the changing
weather, the doctor came at his prey in a
roundabout fashion.

'Archie, I have noticed that there is strong smell of whisky in the room,' he said.

Before he could say another word, the big postie interjected with a tolerant smile.

'I noticed that myself the second I came in but I didnae really like tae say oniething, doctor.'

'But... but... you surely aren't suggesting...' the doctor stuttered.

'Ach, dinnae fash doctor. There's not a chance I'll ever say a word about that outside o this room. I tak the odd drop myself and I can see that a man like you that has to trawl through all that medical phraseology in your books an pamphlets, would likely need a fortifier to get through it. But time's getting on and I must get back tae my rounds. I'll speak to you soon, sir.'

And so saying Archie got up and headed out the front door, picking up his sack of letters as he went. The doctor never let on to anyone else just exactly how he had been so deflected from his purpose.

Another time Archie was on his rounds when Mrs McFarlane, a farmer's wife who was a great advocator of Temperance, spoke much more directly when Archie came to her door.

'Archie, I think that for the sake of your soul

you should be thinking of taking the vow.'
By this she meant the Vow of Temperance,
a process also known as taking the Pledge.
But good Christian as she was she was no match
in theology for our Archie.

'Weel ma'am, I do have to tell you there
is a wee problem there. We fought long an hard
for the true religion in this country and one o the
things that I've read that was close to the heart
of the great thinkers of the Reformation was the
Romanist taking of vows. I am a devout
Protestant and will have nothing to do with such
notions. And as for that ribbon that they give
you to wear I think that is awful close to vanity
and I've no time for such fripperies at all.'
Archie spoke this fluently and clearly for
although he had a few wee 'thochts' already
that morning, he always seemed to wax more
eloquently on religious matters when he was
'a bit warmed up'.

Yet another one of those so concerned with
Archie's soul decided to approach him as he did
his rounds. This was James Soutar a man in his
60s who had spent many years as a colonial
administrator in Egypt and India. He met up
with Archie and began to tell him of his times

abroad. Always of a keen and enquiring mind, Archie was truly interested in Soutar's stories but soon they began to take on a specific colour. He began to tell Archie about just how closely he had worked with the military in his time abroad and that in general had found that the British Army were a fine body of men indeed.

'The only real sadness Archie, was that over the years so many of them did themselves great harm,' he said dolefully.

'Och aye, an how would that have been?' enquired the postie.

'Well, it was the drink you see. Many of them took bad with the heat at first and convinced themselves that they would be better with the help of strong drink. It was sad to see so many of them end up slaves to that evil and pernicious master, both officers and men I might say,' Soutar went on.

'Aye, aye,' said Archie, nodding. 'And where would these lads have been recruited do you know?'

'Oh, they were mainly stalwart Englishmen. Some of them came from around London and a lot of them from the West Country, I believe,' his companion replied.

'I was just thinking that,' Archie went on.
'I didnae think they could have been any of our
Scots lads; they would all ken fine how to handle
their drop, but I have heard that just one or two
glasses of spirits can have an awful effect on
Southerners. And I dare say they weren't
drinking good Scots whisky either.'

the summer house stash

T HE RELATIONSHIP BETWEEN the kirk and drink has long been a complicated one. For every full on fulminator against the demon drink there does seem to have been another one who, if not a supporter of the illicit whisky trade and its importance to Scotland's community economics, was at least an appreciator of whisky itself. This could cause some strain at times. Back in the early 19th century, a newly ordained minister came north to Aberdeenshire to assist an aged incumbent who had been at his post for decades. One evening, shortly after his arrival he was introduced to the assembled elders of the congregation and their wives by his senior partner. After the official business of the evening was over and the two ministers were heading back to the manse, the elder said to the younger, 'Weel, after that I think we could have ourselves a good glass of whisky toddy as a night-cap.'

The young minister was taken aback at this

and didn't know what to say. His companion continued.

'And it's none of your watery government blessed stuff. It's the real thing, a drop of the good old peatreek.'

This was too much for the young man who burst out, 'But minister, is that not against the law? Surely it's prohibited by the Acts of Parliament!'

The older man looked at him with a wee smile and said, 'Ach some of these Acts of Parliament just lose their breath before they get up here to Aberdeenshire.'

In later years, after the old fellow had passed on and the younger had taken up his position, his attitude had changed. One time a visiting minister from Angus who had known the old man and his liking for the spirit of the land asked him, 'Did you ever see himself the waur for drink?'

'I cannae say I've seen him the waur o drink, but no doubt I've seen him the better o't,' was the evasive answer.

This however did not satisfy the visitor, who, glass in hand pushed the question, effectively asking if the old fellow had ever pushed the state of being 'better for a drink' to that happy state of drink-induced unconsciousness. The reply surprised him.

'All I can say is that before that state ever came, I was blind *fou* myself and can testify to nothing.'

There are of course stories of ministers who themselves made peatreek but sometimes the peatreekers themselves took advantage of the minister's place in local society. In the 1850s a new minister arrived at Careston in Forfarshire. This was Robert Moir and his wife had been raised in the Careston manse when her father, Mr James Aikman was minister there. In the course of showing her husband round the house and the grounds she led him into a substantial summer house at the south end of the garden.

'This place could tell you some stories Robert, if it could only speak,' she said with a smile.

'What kind of stories?' asked her husband.

'Well, I wonder if you could find the hidden cellar in here.'

'Why would anyone want a hidden cellar in a summer-house?' asked Robert. His wife let out a ring of laughter. 'Come, come Robert! What would need to be hidden from prying eyes?'

'Are you telling me that they used to hide peatreek in here? Did your father know about it?' he asked, concerned.

'I can only think if I knew abut it, that papa did too,' she replied. 'I do remember him saying that making whisky was one of the few sources of cash for the people round about here and in other parts of the country. He was sympathetic I think. But it would be more of him turning a blind eye than being directly involved.'

'I should hope so,' said her husband. 'Ministers being involved with that business has caused too many scandals down the years.'

'Well, do you think you can find it?'

For the next twenty minutes the minister, watched by his laughing wife tried panel after panel of the wooden walls, trying to locate the secret door. At last she took pity on him and showed him the catch that opened a small door just to the right of the back door which led to a small corridor.

'Would you like to know how we found out about this place?' she asked him with a quizzical look.

'If you want to tell me dearest,' he replied with a smile.

Back when she was child her father had had a servant called John Doig. His job was that of a general assistant and he had work to do in the kirk as well as the manse and people knew him as the Minister's Man. Now one summer it became rather noticeable that a change had come over the steady and reliable John Doig. The minister thought to himself, 'If I didn't know better I'd say he was in love.'

But John was well into his 50s and there was no word of him having any romantic entanglement. Such a thing could hardly be kept secret in a place like Careston. He was generally seen with a smile on his face and always had a pleasant word for whoever he met. Before this he had always been pleasant enough but had been a bit on the taciturn side and most people would have thought themselves lucky to get more than a nod from him. He had also always been a bit pale-skinned but now his skin was suffused with a healthy glow.

This went on for several weeks till one day, about seven in the morning with the sun shining bright, the minister noticed John and another man,

Tam McKidd, a local sawyer, carrying something not far from the summer house.

'Good Morning John,' he said, 'and a good morning to you too Tam. What is this we have here?'

The two men turned bright red and the minister saw that what they were carrying was a small barrel. He had seen barrels like that before.

'John is that what I think it is?' he asked sternly.

Both men looked sheepish.

'Eh… well…' stuttered Doig, looking as if he hoped the very earth beneath his feet would open up and swallow him.

'Right,' said the minister. 'I know exactly what that is. It is a barrel full of whisky. Where did you get it, and where exactly are you taking it?'

The story tumbled out. One day in May while cleaning the summer house, John had leaned against the door of the secret hiding place and it had opened. Looking in he saw the barrels and at once he knew what they were. He had in his youth been involved for a couple of years with the making of peatreek. Realising that it had probably been there for years he could hardly wait to taste the stuff. It exceeded his expectations; the long years in the barrel had let it mature into what was the finest drop of spirits that he had ever tasted.

He had been quietly tippling away for several months having taken some of the barrels to his own home in the in village under the cover of darkness. But after a while he had begin to feel guilty at having this secret supply and had told some of his friends including Tam McKidd. They had all been drinking whisky nearly every night for the past couple of months and, truth to tell, most days the morning porridge had been supplemented with a drop or ten of the barley bree. Little wonder John Doig had been going around with a smile on his face!

'Well John, I am sorry but you know what I have to do don't you?' said the minister. A crestfallen John simply nodded.

So the local gauger was summoned and led to the secret hidey-hole where the whisky had been hidden. However, apart from the anker, or barrel that John and Tam had been carrying off, there was only one other and the minister realised that there would be little point now in asking his man how many barrels he had actually found. The gauger was a little disappointed but nowhere near as much as John, Tam and the rest of their cronies. Mr Aikman was a sympathetic man and he kept John on as Minister's Man, but from then on it became a talking point in the area that John Doig was a rather sad character.

It wasn't long after this when John and his friends gathered in the local tavern one night and were sipping at whisky they had had to pay for – which was not a patch on the stuff from the summer house – when Tam asked John about his time making whisky in his youth.

'How many drams would you take in a normal day making the stuff?' he inquired.

'Och now,' replied John. 'To tell you the God's truth the most I can mind of having taken in a day was five and twenty glasses, besides the usual allowance.' The usual allowance was half a dozen glasses so we can be pretty sure that the peatreekers were happy in their work! But as John pointed out, it was hard work and you spent a great deal of time out in the open air, often travelling along difficult country to avoid the gaugers so a wee glass or ten of the whisky was needed to keep you going.

the clean shaven minister

A LOT HAS BEEN SAID, sung and written about the glorious beauty of Scotland over the centuries. Painters and poets have thrilled at the exquisite and dramatic scenery that can be found in so many different parts of this wonderful land. A flavour of how Scots themselves see the land can be seen in the weel-kennt tale of God and St Peter.

God called Peter in one day when he was creating the earth and said, 'Look Pete, this is wee cracker of a country I'm making here. It has beautiful, soaring mountains, sheltered lovely glens, the purest water anywhere on earth and air so pure you could bottle and sell it. The mountains are full of beautiful red deer, the rivers with salmon and in the lowlands there is lush, rich grass for all sorts of livestock.'

'I presume you'll be putting people in here?' queried Peter.

'Oh aye,' said God. 'They will be a proud, adventurous, creative and friendly lot I reckon.'

'But, don't you think you're spoiling them a bit with all this?' asked the Big Fisherman.

'Och, just you wait till you see their neighbours.'

Now it is true that we Scots do like to take pot-shots at the English now and again, but they are as nothing to how the Glaswegians and Edinburghers talk of each other, so just grin and bear it if you are from the lesser part of this fine island.

To offset the undoubted majesty of the country there is of course the weather. The depressing months of little daylight, and those filled with what seems an endless variety of permutations of cold, wind, sleet, rain and snow; some years seem to last forever. Along with this general inclemency we have various forms of illness. We have already considered the Buchan method of how to deal with the sniffles, but here is a variation on the story of the need to defend one's body against the incursions of the cold, flu and other nasties.

It took place over a hundred years ago, at a time when virtually everybody in all the rural parishes of Scotland was a regular churchgoer. It is all too easy to paint this as a form of fanaticism, but it cannot be denied that the kirk held communities together in ways we now see were beneficial indeed. The central importance of the kirk to community life was obvious, but it also brought some limitations, particularly to ministers. As we have seen already, there were more than a few ministers who well understood that whisky was itself one of God's blessings, but this was not a universally held point of view.

There was once a minister, himself a McDrouthy who had strayed from the well-worn path of his ancestors and entered the kirk, who was not one of those who fulminated excessively against the demon drink. He had, on occasion, when propriety suggested it, taken a drink or two, but by the standards of his forebears he was abstemiousness personified. At the time of our story he was a man in his forties, still single, and had a housekeeper called Janet who was truly ancient. Nobody knew exactly how old Janet was but she had 'done' for three previous ministers in the same manse and had a particular view of the universe. This was a narrow-minded view that was matched only by her pride in her own

station as housekeeper to the minister –
though she would have been mortified to
have had her feelings described as pride.
That was a sin, and Janet was a body who
was against sin in all its forms. However she
was a very efficient housekeeper and a first-class,
if somewhat pedestrian, cook. The minister
appreciated her skills and was careful never
to upset her.

One time the minister had come down
with a nasty dose of the sniffles. It went on
for weeks and at last he called in the local
doctor, a close friend with whom he sometimes
went walking in the nearby hills, something
which brought them great pleasure.

After a cursory examination the doctor
said, 'Well then, I reckon you have a bad case
of the cold. It's in both your head and your chest
but I think we can fix you up.'

'Och, that would be just grand,' replied the
minister. 'I am fed up to the back teeth feeling
this bad and this runny nose is a real bother.'

'Aye, aye,' said his friend. 'I reckon all
you need it have a hot toddy every evening
before you go to bed. That should shift it
in a day or so.'

'A toddy!' was the shocked reply. 'That's made with whisky.'

'Well, aye,' the doctor retorted. 'You can make it with brandy or rum if you have a mind to it, but whisky is the best.'

'Och! No, no, no! You don't understand.' The minister was clearly worried as he spoke. 'There has never been a drop of alcohol in this manse in all Janet's time. She would be mortified if she knew I was drinking strong spirits. And you know she talks daily to her four sisters in the village. I wouldn't like to be the subject of gossip about drinking you know.'

'Aha, I see,' mused the doctor. 'We might have a way round this. I really do think that the toddy would do you good, man.'

'What do you suggest?' asked the Reverend McDrouthy.

'I take it you shave of a night?'

'Well, not every night, but two or three times a week, aye,' said McDrouthy.

'All right then, I'll drop by later today with a bottle, you can lock it in your desk. Just ask Janet for some shaving water before you go to bed, Use some of the hot water to make yourself a toddy and shave with the rest and she'll be none the wiser,' explained the doctor.

'Och, that seems a bit underhand,' the minister said.

'Never mind that, it'll do you good. Now I'm off but I'll be back later with a bottle,' said the doctor heading for the door.

Sure enough the doctor was back later in the day with, not just one but a couple of bottles in his big doctor's bag. These he left with the minister and went off on his rounds of the nearby countryside. The following day he was called away to visit a relative who was very ill indeed and didn't come back for almost a month. He had just come back to the village when he ran into Janet outside the Post Office.

'Good, day Janet. Are you well?' he asked, doffing his hat.

'Och, thank you very much doctor. I am just as ever I was. Is this you back now?'

'Aye, aye. I'll not be travelling again for a good bit I hope. But tell me Janet, when I left the minister was not too well, is he any better?' he asked.

'I suppose you could say that, but I think

he is coming over strange,' replied the old lady with a wee sigh.

'Yes? Janet, what do you mean?'

'Well, he was never a man of vanity, sir, but lately he seems to be thinking a lot more about his appearance,' she replied.

'What exactly do you mean?' he asked.

'Before he would shave once or twice a week – on a Wednesday and a Saturday. Nowadays he just has to have a shave every night of the week.'

the lesson

OW DOWN THE YEARS there were many men of the cloth who liked a drop of the peatreek. There were others however who saw strong drink as essentially sinful and there have been several periods in Scotland over the past couple of hundred years where Temperance has had a lot of support. There are those who will tell you that Winston Churchill after being ejected from the parliamentary seat of Dundee in 1922 was most deeply hurt by the fact that his opponent, Neddy Scrymgeour, was the leader of the Scottish Prohibition Party.

Ministers down the years have often railed against the evils of drink and there was one such fellow back in the mid 1850s who had been declaiming against whisky in particular. His parish was on the edge of one of our great cities and was well known for being the entry point for whisky brought down from the Highlands. He cast up at his congregation about their habits time and again, and truth be told there was a fair amount of drink being taken about the place. But, given the hard work

that most people had to do, and of course the
changeable weather, a drink or two was needed
by many just to get through the day. However,
this minister was not a man to admit defeat
and he decided that what was needed to wean
his congregation off their liking for the peatreek
was a practical display. So one Sunday, as the
gathered community settled down for what they
were sure would be another hell and brimstone
attack on their tippling habits, the minister
surprised them.

'I have told you all on many an occasion
that your sinful ways are doing you no good,
either here on earth or in the life to come.
Today I will show you precisely why.'

He reached below the pulpit and pulled
out two glasses. One was a clear liquid and
the other a beautiful shining amber colour
that most of the congregation recognised
immediately. Whatever was going on?
Was the minister actually allowing the
cratur under the roof of his church? Strange
behaviour indeed. The entire congregation
was intrigued and sat up, their eyes fixed on their
spiritual shepherd.

'Here,' he said. 'We have two glasses.

On my right, the great gift of our Creator –
water, Adam's ale, that comes to us in pure
stream from the rocks of the Highlands to
our north. On my left, something entirely
different that also comes down from the
north but has no purity at all; this is what
the unenlightened among us call *uisge beatha*,
but the water of life it is not. It is a foul brew,
the work of Satan, a pernicious and poisonous
potion that destroys families and is much more
the water of death! Oft have I warned you of
its evil power and foulness. Now I will show
you the difference between water and foul
whisky. Between good and evil!'

Reaching inside his waistcoat pocket
he brought out a worm. The congregation
took a sharp breath as if one. What was
going on here? Whisky in the church and
now a worm? Queer doings indeed.

With a flourish the minister dropped
the worm into the water. There it wriggled
around for a few moments before he fished
it out with his fingers. Then holding it high
above his head he turned so that all in the
church could get a clear view of the little creature
wriggling in between his fingers. Then with

a flourish worthy of a stage magician he
dropped the creature into the glass of whisky.
The worm hit the liquid, went rigid, and
dropped in a lifeless crumple to the bottom
of the glass.

'There!' he roared. 'There you see the
evidence with your own eyes. Now...' and
he looked around the whole congregation
with a masterful look. 'What does this tell you?'

The assembled locals sat still in silence till,
at last a small quizzical voice rang out from
the back of the kirk.

'If you've got worms, drink whisky?'

a good shift

SOMETIMES CELEBRATION can get a little over the top and if the chosen drink is whisky then sometimes – but only sometimes – things can get just a wee bit out of hand. We have had occasion to take note of the importance of the kirk in Scottish life in the past and it is something that is difficult to overestimate. This was not just a matter of everybody being a Bible-bashing, pleasure-hating Holy Wullie, it was to a great extent a matter of community. The kirk was at the heart of rural and village life and when people tended to be working six days a week, Sunday was a day not only of rest but was a chance for the community to come together, to exchange news (and gossip), to arrange future communal activities and to plan weddings. The community functioned round the church.

So when a church was burnt down, it wasn't just the minister but the entire community that was affected. This happened one time at Meigle in Strathmore, between the Sidlaw Hills on the north bank of the River Tay and the Grampian mountain range. Nowadays Meigle is a quiet wee place probably best known for its museum of Pictish Symbol Stones but back in the 1860s it was a bustling community serving a large population living on the surrounding farms and estates. Once the initial shock of the church burning down was over, the community rallied and the church was soon restored and repaired. Now we all know about the ministers and just how important their role was, but there were others in the kirk community who were also pillars of the community. These were the Elders; to be elected an Elder of the Kirk by your congregation was a great mark of respect, and though there were of course those who let such office go to their heads, the main Elders were people who their peers considered decent and capable human beings. They were of course drawn from the community at large and were really no different than the rest. Naturally this meant that there were many kirk Elders who liked a dram, or two. Once the Meigle kirk had been restored to its former glory – well… really it was rather austere; we *are* talking Presbyterianism here – the Elders held a meeting. The reason for this

was said to have been to discuss the 'new' church
but the fact that they chose to hold their meeting
in the local inn meant everybody knew the main
theme of the evening was celebration not
deliberation. And so it proved.

The first few toasts were to 'a job well
done', 'our duties fulfilled' and the like but
soon as the whisky began to take hold it was
'health and happiness' and of course the old
standby 'Here's tae us, wha's like us' and it's
inevitable response, 'Damn few, an they're
aw deid!' As the night wore on, jokes began
to be told, and the nature of agricultural
humour was such that it was just as well the
minister himself had left after the first toast.
Songs were sung, some of a bawdy nature,
in short the Elders were having a grand old
time. After about three hours, with the
midsummer sun still shining behind drifting
clouds, the group decided to go out and take
a look at their handiwork. Then something
happened. How it happened no one knows.
Why it happened... well, whisky is a
powerful beast.

As they stood there swaying, and appraising
their kirk, somebody suggested that it looked

as if it was too far to the west. The idea
immediately took hold. All agreed the church
somehow had ended up a couple of feet west
of where it should be. What was to be done?
Now these were all practical men, men to
whom hard work was certainly no stranger
and men who were well used to problem solving
and they had had a good deal of whisky.
So a decision was made.

This is how it came about that one
midsummer's night, the assembled Elders
of Meigle kirk got in a line against the west
wall of the building, put their shoulders and
heaved with all their might! Maybe some of
them looked up and saw the clouds moving
and with the whisky churning their brains
thought they and the kirk were moving.
Whatever it was that convinced them, after
a few minutes of extreme endeavour a halt
was called. Some gasping, with their hands
on their knees and their heads down, others
taking off their hats to wipe the sweat from
their brows, the Elders stood back to admire
their work.

'Aye a guid job well done,' said one and
the other nodded and murmured in assent.

All were satisfied that they had accomplished just what they had set out to do and restored the church to its rightful position. As one commented, they had put in a good shift. There was nothing else to be done but to seal their efforts with a dram. So they all trooped off back to the inn to continue their religious celebration.

enough is enough

WHISKY IS OF COURSE associated with fun. It is something people drink when they want to enjoy themselves and down the years there have been many instances of behaviour that, while perhaps not too funny to the people involved at the time, have found their way into the story tradition. Many of these types of story (it should come as no surprise) rely on over-consumption of the nippy sweeties for their punch line.

Now back in the days before such ultra-modern inventions as the motor-car, the telephone, or even the steam train had been thought up, the social life of Scotland relied on the trusty communication methods of Shanks's pony and/or the horse. Obviously the majority of people walked wherever they wanted to go but the lairds, the landowning class, could afford to travel by horse and in many instances even by horse and carriage. But of course until the 19th century much of the road system of Scotland was, to be blunt, rubbish. Many of them, even between quite substantial towns and villages were little more than dirt tracks. This was especially true in places like the Highlands and in Galloway.

In Galloway, as elsewhere, it was common for lairds to visit the others' houses and while this often entailed decent food it invariably meant that there would be a fair amount of drink taken. In the late 18th century it was common for every piece of business done – at whatever level – to be accompanied by a drink or two to seal the deal. Nowadays, perhaps too many of the medical profession blame drink for all sorts of ills, forgetting that we have an ancestral tendency, and perhaps even a traditional obligation, to drink. And back in those days when lairds kept servants on hand to help carry overnight guests to their beds from the dining table, drunkenness was not only tolerated but expected. Among the common people things were not quite so bad due to the fact that most folk could not afford to be so bibulous, but on those occasions where drink was on hand, it was drunk – and so were the people. It is well to remember that there are still a great many human societies where, amongst those who have to work hard for a living, a 'livener' is often taken with breakfast or morning coffee.

It happened one time in the faraway past on the coast of Galloway, south of Dalbeattie that a laird rode over to a neighbouring laird's house for the evening. Behind him on his horse sat his good lady, Jeanie. The way was rough and even if they had had a carriage it would have done them little good, but they were used to it and it was only a journey of around four miles. By this stage in their lives neither of the visitors was in the first flush of youth, and their host and his good lady were friends of a great many years' standing. The food was good, the conversation to everyone's satisfaction and the drink flowed like water, especially the whisky. Now in those days it was often the custom to vary the whisky over an evening. Not as in today's sophisticated world, with single malts from different distilleries, and even different vintages of the same single malt, but instead between hot and cold. The hot version was of course toddy and a copious amount of the stuff was necked over the evening.

At last the visiting laird decided it was time to return home; despite the heartfelt entreaties

to stay over, he had things to do the following
day and insisted on leaving. This of course
meant a few more drinks. The ancient Highland
hospitality of the *Deoch an Dorus* was
impossible to ignore. This was the drink
of parting, literally the drink at the door
but properly done included a few more slugs
of whisky before the door was reached.
And given that it was cold night these last
few drinks were all of toddy. It was with some
difficulty that the visiting wife was sat behind
her husband, and as soon as she was astride
the horse, she was drifting in and out of sleep.
After a last farewell they set off home over
the moors in the dark night.

Luckily the horse knew the way well.
By the time they were half way along the
four mile journey, Jeanie was sound asleep
and her husband was beginning to nod off
himself. He tried to keep himself awake by
singing, but whatever song he started he
soon forgot the words and it was only a
matter of time before he too fell sound asleep
on the horse's back, his wife's arms still clasped
firmly around his ample waist.

The next thing he knew he was at his own
front door.

'Laird, Laird!' he heard his servant cry. 'Where's the gudewife?'

He became fully awake and realised that his wife was no longer behind him!

Rousing the rest of his servants and the workers at the farm close by, a search party was arranged. He himself and his grieve, or farm manager, and three others all set off on horseback. The laird was in a right state. Falling from horseback had killed more than few people in his experience and he was sore afraid for his Jeanie. They galloped back along the road torches held high as they rode.

They came to the ford across the Urr water just where it met the sea and by the light of the torches they could see what looked like a bundle of clothes lying half in the water. As her husband dismounted and ran to her side the tide which had just turned, began to trickle into her mouth. As he bent to raise her up his relief was enormous for he could see she was breathing. But then she murmured something he was never to forget; spitting out the salt water, she slurred the words, 'No, no, no. Not another drop – neither hot nor cold.'

the competitive spirit

VISITORS TO SCOTLAND often comment on our affection for our national tipple and back in the 1730s, Edmund Burt was one of the first. He was a quartermaster with General Wade who was developing a network of roads that were designed to open up the Highlands. While this was a specifically military endeavour, intending to allow the rapid movement of British Army troops to trouble hot-spots in the clan lands, the roads had other consequences. They were of course first used by the Highlanders of Bonnie Prince Charlie's army in 1745 to move quickly to central Scotland and meet up with their Lowland fellow Jacobites, taking the Government totally by surprise. Another side-effect of the Wade roads was that they were a great help to the distribution of Highland whisky – of the illicit kind. It was a way to access growing markets in the central belt of Scotland and beyond.

Burt himself was a bit disapproving of the Scots' fondness for whisky and suspicious of some of the claims made for the wondrous nectar. He refused to accept the Highlanders' statements that whisky had less effect in the rarefied air of the mountains than it did in the Lowlands and believed that any who drank too much of the stuff (what is too much anyway? We all know whisky makes you go to sleep before you have had too much, don't we?) were no better than barbarians, whatever they are. He was shocked to hear the estimate of the customs officer at Stornoway that one hundred and twenty families got through 4,000 gallons of spirits in a year, averaging out about 35 gallons per family. Well, they did have big families back then. He was further taken aback at the fact that children from seven or eight were regularly given what we would now think of as trebles. He mentions in passing they not only mixed it with honey and hot water but also with milk and honey – which would no doubt be more palatable for the children and invalids.

While Burt was definitely not in favour of what he saw as excessive drinking, some of his fellow officers saw things a little differently. One time a group of four of them decided to have a bit of a whisky

drinking match with some of the local lads.
The officers were all young men and full of
that mad bravado that sometimes can pass
with the advancing of years. They saw it as
a matter of the honour of the British Army
itself to show that they could keep up with
these half-savage creatures of the mountains.
So, in a wee clachan in the heart of the
Highlands the drinking match took place.
As ever there were a great many toasts –
which in itself caused a bit of a problem as
the Highlanders were not too keen to toast
a German king, and the officers would commit
treason if they toasted the 'king over the water'.
However, conviviality was the watchword of
the evening and more general toasts to the
health of the company, the ladies etc. were
more than adequate. All went well for a while
but as the evening wore on and the pace of
drinking did not flag at all, the army officers
began to suffer a bit. One of them began to
surreptitiously pour his whisky on the floor
when no one was looking but his (more
honourable?) companions kept at it, throwing
back glass after glass of the aqua vitae to match
their kilted companions. It is perhaps down

to Burt's natural rectitude that we do not know exactly how the evening ended up, though we can imagine.

What he did tell us was the effect the night's drinking had on his fellow officers. Apart from the one who cheated – and afterwards he was a bit ashamed of this unsportsmanlike conduct – the British Army lads had a casualty rate of one hundred percent. One of them was stricken the following day with gout – a nasty limb-rotting pestilence that can often render even moderate drinkers immobile – and he had it the rest of his days. The second brave fellow was gripped by a dangerous, life-threatening fever which lasted for some time and does sound like alcohol poisoning. The third one, however, had the oddest experience of all. According to Burt, he lost not only all his hair but his skin as well! That must have been some fine brew they were drinking that night. And the natives? Well, they were up and about at their work the next morning.

a man of style

ONE OF THE BEST-KENNT Scottish characters from the period around the turn of the 17th and 18th centuries is Rob Roy McGregor. This is probably because Sir Walter Scott, the Great Romantic, wrote about him, but Rob Roy is in many ways symbolic of a whole swathe of Scottish Highland culture and tradition. First he was a McGregor, an unfortunate clan who were hounded for centuries by both successive Kings of Scots and their sworn enemies the Clan Campbell, a tribe with an eye for the main chance if ever there was one. The McGregors were driven off their ancestral lands as early as the 16th century and often forced to adopt other clan names as their own name was made illegal in 1603. At one point the Campbells were even said to breed greyhounds that could smell out McGregors having been raised on the breast milk of McGregor women captured for that explicit purpose. Given that the clans of the Highlands were warrior based, it is little wonder that the landless McGregors became known for their fighting prowess, honed through continual resistance against those who literally wanted to wipe them from the face of the earth.

Rob Roy exemplifies many characteristics of the Highland warrior. People still argue over whether he was a cattle-drover or a cattle thief. In truth even as late as the 18th century the distinction is almost meaningless in Highland terms. It had been the practice since at least the Iron Age, nearly two millennia earlier, for the clans to raid each other, to 'lift' cattle. This act was not considered theft within Highland society, no matter what they thought in the Lowlands or in the capital, Edinburgh. Someone who raised his own cattle was perfectly capable of raiding others' herds and of course often defending his own. It was a part of tribal warrior life and as the modern world inched into the Highlands, the old ways often clashed with what was 'the modern way'. Another typical Highland aspect of Rob Roy was that he had both sworn enemies and loyal friends. The relationships between marauding clans, which could include both inter-marriage and blood-feuds meant that there were often very complicated links of obligation, friendship

and downright hatred between different clans,
to say nothing of the problems that could happen
within a single clan!

So it was in 1717 that Rob Roy ended
up being a prisoner of the Duke of Atholl
at Logierait in Perthshire. Logierait was
where Atholl used to hold his local court
and Rob had turned up at the Duke's request
thinking they were to discuss a cattle deal.
However, when he got there he was surrounded
by an armed group of Atholl's clansmen and
thrown into jail. He was, as they say, black
affronted. He had come of his own accord
and been treacherously thrown in jail.
He considered this to be a highly dishonourable
act on the part of the Duke. Like many of
his sort, the Duke was keen to put the loyalties
of the clan past behind him, (except when they
served his needs) and he was a firm supporter
of centralised government and the law, which
he well understood would never work against
his interests. He thus sent word to Edinburgh
that he had Rob Roy McGregor in custody
knowing fine well that there were a number
of charges pending against McGregor in the
High Court. At first he asked for troops to

be sent to convey Rob Roy to the capital for trial, but then changed his mind and decided to send the prisoner with a group of his own men. This delayed matters a bit and Rob Roy, never a man to let an advantage slip, began to make the effort to get on with his jailers. He had been arrested on a variety of charges but, even though he had been carrying a full purse, expecting to be buying cattle, his money wasn't taken.

With money in his pocket and time on his hands, what would you expect a fine Highland gentleman like Rob to do? He sent for whisky. And being as he was known as a generous soul, he didn't just send for a bottle, he sent for half a dozen. Now these were none of your wee government approved, namby-pamby 70 centilitre bottles that the *cratur* is marketed in these days, these were the old greybeards that held between two and four times what modern bottles do. Then again we should remember that people who lived much of their life in the open air, who were used to walking rather than driving and led very active lives, had a capacity for drinking that would shame a judge, if that were ever possible. And of course when the whisky arrived Rob insisted that his

jailers took a dram. They themselves would
have considered it a grave insult to their prisoner
to refuse. So a couple of greybeards were
polished off the first night between Rob and
the three burly jailers keeping an eye on him.
The following night the same crew did in four
more and on the third day Rob sent out for
another half dozen flagons.

Now the two previous nights had been
a great delight for the jailers – two Robertsons
brothers, and a Donnachie who were part of
the Duke of Atholl's bodyguard. Like all
Highlanders, they were addicted to storytelling
and singing and Rob Roy, like so many warriors
who attained significant reputations, was a man
who could tell a story and carry a song.
The three lads were looking forward to a third
evening's entertainment when the bottles arrived
from a nearby inn. They knew that Rob was
due to be sent to Edinburgh the day after the
next but had decided not to let him know till
the last minute, just in case. However, Rob
had no need of their intelligence; his plans
were already well in motion.

Rob had earlier asked permission to write
a letter to his wife. Knowing fine well that once

he was in Edinburgh there was a very good
chance that Rob would soon be dancing the
gallows jig, the lads had readily agreed. So it
was, just after the second greybeard of whisky
had been emptied, that the messenger arrived
to get the letter from Rob.

'Is it all right if I have wee word with
the lad?' asked Rob. 'I'd like to pass on some
private instructions for him to give to my wife.'

The elder of the Robertson brothers agreed
that that would be fine and as he opened the
third bottle, with his friends closely watching
him, Rob moved towards the door where the
messenger was standing. He talked to the
messenger in a soft voice and the man left.
The three lads were concentrating on getting
their glasses topped up as Rob stood at the door.
He moved away and back twice, his jailers
hardly bothering to watch concentrating as
they were on the fine liquor they were drinking.
Rob had earlier realised that his horse had been
tethered just abut 50 yards from the jail and after
a couple of minutes lounging at the door he
turned to see that none of the jailers was looking
directly at him. Like a flash he ran and jumped in
the saddle of his horse and pulling the reins free,

turned the creature round, kicked with his heels and was off.

By the time the half befuddled guards were aware of what had happened Rob Roy was well on the way home. Like his ancestors he loved the whisky, but was never a slave to it and well knew how to use it to his advantage.

mcdrouthy and the sheriff's officer

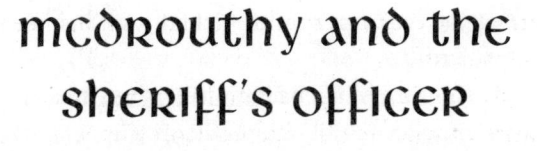N THE OLD DAYS when chiefs were still chiefs and the leaders of their clans, before they had transmogrified into that pale imitation of English gentry, there were more than a few sharp characters amongst them. Being as they were heirs to centuries of self-sufficiency in economic terms, some of them were none too responsible when it came it money. After all hadn't their ancestors been living off the land since the time of the Flood? When questioned as to this belief that the Highlanders had survived the Great Flood of Noah the standard reply was simply, 'did you ever hear of a West Coast man who didn't have a boat?'

Some of the chiefs it would have to be admitted were, as they say, a bit fly and living much of their time on the ancestral lands in the Highlands they were more than capable of running up a fair amount of debt when they did venture down to Edinburgh or even London.

One such character was the ancestral chief of
the McDrouthys before the clan was scattered
to bar-rooms and shebeens across the globe.
On one trip to the capital he had ordered
a vast amount of good claret and brandy to
be delivered back up to his ancestral home
then had gone off on a tour of Edinburgh's
finest emporia. The upshot was he bought
a very expensive pair of customised pistols,
several top class suits of clothing in the
Highland style and four or five pairs of boots.
He then headed off back to the mountains and
the glens, and the bills were sent out in due
course. Nothing happened. A few weeks after
that the city merchants who had catered to
McDrouthy's expensive tastes sent out a further
round of bills for goods and services rendered.
Nothing happened. Now, as he had spent
a great deal of money which he apparently
didn't have, the various affronted shopkeepers
and artisans, considerably out of pocket,
got together to try and sort the matter out.
It was obvious to them that this Highland
brigand had absolutely no intention of settling
his debts. This was an affront to their pockets
as much, if not more than, to their combined

sense of propriety. McDrouthy's sense of propriety, such as it was, had developed from his ancestors, all of whom had been making predatory raids on other clans and occasionally the Lowlands for centuries, so he could be said to be behaving in a time-honoured manner. Either way he wasn't much bothered.

The situation continued for a while and at last the Edinburgh merchants lost patience. They decided to have the law on McDrouthy. Accordingly they hired a lawyer, swore out the necessary affidavits and a sheriff's officer was sent to the McDrouthy ancestral lands to serve a writ.

By this time the Highlands were, supposedly, pacified and the sheriff's officer, with a legal writ in his possession was confident that he would have little or no trouble – after all hadn't he been assured that McDrouthy was a gentleman? However, a Highland gentleman and a Lowland gentleman were not exactly the same thing. When he reached McDrouthy's home, a fortified tower house with a stunning view over the beautiful River Lochy, the officer was met at the door by The McDrouthy himself.

'Good afternoon,' said the chief taking the

man by the hand and shaking it forcefully. 'Welcome to the land of my fathers. It is lovely isn't it?'

Without giving the man a chance to reply McDrouthy went on. 'It has long been the tradition hereabouts for a visitor to have a drink on arrival. You will take a dram will you not?'

The officer didn't have a chance to refuse for one of McDrouthy's clansmen was immediately at his elbow pressing a large bumper of whisky into his hand.

'A toast!' cried McDrouthy. 'Here's to health, wealth and prosperity for all of Scotland.'

And saying this he downed in one the contents of the glass he was holding in his own hand. The bemused Lowlander felt he had no choice but to do the same so he tossed off the full glass of whisky in one. The effects were instantaneous. His cheeks flushed, a sweat broke out on his brow and it was with some difficulty that he managed not to cough.

'Weel done,' said his host signalling to his henchman to re-fill both their glasses. This done, McDrouthy immediately downed the second glass and the sheriff's officer followed suit.

'Come on in, come on in. A thousand welcomes to my humble home. You will stay the night won't you?' said McDrouthy, ushering the bemused man into the house.

The sheriff's officer was about to state his business at this point but McDrouthy just carried on talking as he led his guest into the house. The poor mannie couldn't get a word in edgeways and before having him shown to his room McDrouthy called for two more large bumpers of whisky. Now the sheriff's officer was an Edinburgh man and was well used to drinking a significant amount of claret but he was not used to the *uisge beatha*. And truth to tell it was the very best of the amber nectar – *treas-tarraing* – the thrice distilled favourite of the Highlander and to say it had a kick would be like suggesting night follows day. Even after three, admittedly large, glasses of this delightful liquid he had a bit of a glow on. Now, he was a man of some experience and reckoned that he knew what McDrouthy was doing; he was trying to get him drunk. Very well, he would play along and simply hand over the writ in the morning before he left.

Telling him he would see him at dinner time,

McDrouthy went off and the officer was shown
to his rather spartan room. There was a bed,
a big old chest, a table and a chair and on
the table there was another bottle of whisky.
Wisely, the officer decided against taking more
of the amber nectar before the evening meal.
He thought he would just lie down for a little,
and promptly fell asleep. He was awakened
a while later to be told that dinner was about
to be served and went down to join his host
in the big hall of the tower. Here he was regaled
with a meal of salmon and roast venison
accompanied of course by more and more
whisky. There was a retainer standing at his
elbow and every time he drank his whisky his
glass was refilled. McDrouthy too had a man
with a bottle standing at his elbow but the
sheriff officer did not realise that this was full
of water (well, half full – the rest being whisky
of course). So whisky after whisky was drunk
and a great deal of food taken as the evening
wore on. It didn't take long for the officer to
begin to drift off to sleep in his chair. While he
was dozing, McDrouthy gave a signal to one
of his clansmen who went off to do what had
already been arranged.

Some time later the sheriff's officer was awakened and shown to his bed. In truth he was half carried, but through it all he thought he had held out well and would sort things out in the morning.

It was the middle of the morning and McDrouthy was sitting by the fire in his own great hall when the door burst open. There stood his guest, ashen-faced and trembling.

'My good lad, what ever is wrong with you?' asked McDrouthy rising from his chair and going to his guest. The man looked at him with his eyes almost popping from his head.

'Wha...wha... what is that outside my window?' he blurted out.

'Outside your window?' asked McDrouthy acting puzzled.

'Yes, outside my... my window. Hanging from that tree,' stuttered the Lowlander.

'Och that,' laughed McDrouthy. 'That's just a man they sent up here from Edinburgh a few days ago with some kind of summons for me.'

At this the sheriff's officer went even whiter and ran from the room. He barely reached the front door before he was violently sick.

McDrouthy followed him to the door where the man turned and said, 'I am s...s...sorry but I have some people to see. At once,' and he headed off not even waiting for his breakfast.

McDrouthy wandered round to the back of the tower and looked up at the straw man hanging from the tree and laughed, before heading back indoors for what he thought was a richly deserved dram.

the water of life,
right enough

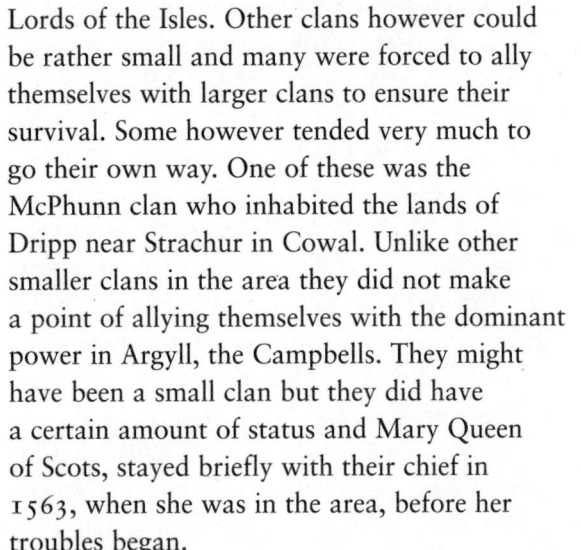OW IN THE SCOTTISH HIGHLANDS in the Middle Ages there were many different clans. Some, like the MacDonalds, were so numerous that they we split up into different clans, even if they all claimed descent from the Lords of the Isles. Other clans however could be rather small and many were forced to ally themselves with larger clans to ensure their survival. Some however tended very much to go their own way. One of these was the McPhunn clan who inhabited the lands of Dripp near Strachur in Cowal. Unlike other smaller clans in the area they did not make a point of allying themselves with the dominant power in Argyll, the Campbells. They might have been a small clan but they did have a certain amount of status and Mary Queen of Scots, stayed briefly with their chief in 1563, when she was in the area, before her troubles began.

Not long after this there was a chief of the

McPhunns who had an unfortunate brush
with the law. This chief, Roderick, despite
the limited number of men at his disposal,
was heavily involved with the traditional clan
practice of raiding. This raiding, which had
been going on between the various tribes since
time immemorial, was generally focused on
lifting cattle but McPhunn had developed a
speciality in the lifting of sheep. Because of
where he lived, the optimum method of going
on raids or *spreachs* was by water. To this end
he had a large flat-bottomed boat which he
could land on virtually any beach making it
very easy to lift any livestock that was nearby.
Sheep of course were much easier to handle in
a boat than cattle and McPhunn became very
successful at blagging sheep. Generally he would
keep them on his own lands for a while then sell
them on. Now in the days of the *cateran*,
the Highland raiders, it was generally a strict
law that you did not raid lands close to your
own home. Raiders would travel for days to
lift cattle and often would go a hundred miles
or more. Given the geography of Argyll however,
the McPhunns, being able to get in and out
of shoreline pastures at great speed, grew a bit

cocky and began to raid a bit too close to home. This meant of course that it was only a matter of time before neighbouring clans figured out what they were up to.

Now, one of the things that changed Highland life in the later Middle Ages was the use of the law. For hundreds, if not thousands of years, matters were settled by the sword or amicable discussion, but as time passed and central government continued to try and control what they saw as the 'lawless' Highlands,' various chiefs began to use the law to their own advantage. If you could get the King and his advisers to issue you with letters of fire and sword against your enemies, you could attack them knowing that you had the backing of the government and could call on others to help implement what was, after all, the law of the land.

So it was that some of the other clans in Argyll went to the court in Edinburgh to have McPhunn brought to justice. Because of his independence Roderick didn't have any friends at court to plead his case, nor did he have enough money to bribe the relevant officials, which was of course a well established practice. While it is possible that he may have had the cash, given his sheep-raiding success, he did not know how to go about working the system. Also, because he did not have influential friends, he did not even know that he had been targeted; it was a complete surprise to him and his men, when one day a large company of armed men descended on Dripp and took Roderick into custody. They had chosen their time carefully, when they knew there would be only a few men about and there were simply too many of them to be resisted. The upshot of it was that McPhunn was tied up, thrown across a horse and taken off to Inverary, the seat of the Campbells. Never having bothered to make friends with MacAilen Mor, the chief of Clan Campbell, Roderick's fate was a foregone conclusion. It was Campbell himself who was the judge and he knew fine well that McPhunn had taken many of his own sheep. With no-one to speak for him and there being no real threat from the small numbers of the McPhunn clan, the outcome was inevitable. Death by hanging.

At this time Roderick was a man in his 40s, but he had a young wife named Mary and she

had only recently given birth to a son.
Fearing for the worst she made her way
to Inverary in the flat bottomed boat, manned
by her husband's closest friend, Angus Dubh
and half a dozen more of his companions in
crime. Truth to tell, they were all a bit reluctant
to come so close to the gallows from which
they could so easily end up hanging themselves.
Still, she was the chief's wife and they wanted
to bring his body back for burial alongside his
ancestors at Dripp. They hoped that MacAilean
Mor would be satisfied with having executed
their chief. With Roderick's son less than a year
old and still breast-feeding, Campbell clearly
thought the chances of the McPhunns causing
any more trouble, with no prospect of having
an effective chief for many years, were nil.

As the mourning clansmen and their chief's
wife made their fateful journey their minds
were full of the good times they had had with
their chief. Not only had they been successful
raiders but McPhunn had always made sure
that they had the very best food and, more
importantly, drink. He had long been making
his own *uisge beatha* in a pot-still in the cellar
of his house and its quality was of the very

finest. It had long been the habit to carry
a large flagon of this glorious golden nectar
on their raids and as ever the flagon was in
the boat, full.

The boat arrived at Inverary just after
McPhunn had been hanged and, satisfied
with his day's work MacAilean Mor was
gracious enough to let the arriving McPhunns
cut down the body to take it home for burial.

The grieving clansmen cut down their
chief under the watchful eyes of Campbell's
heavily armed body guard while Roderick's
grief-stricken wife looked on, clutching her
young son to her breast. Through her tears
she looked at her husband's corpse and the
fact that he looked so like himself in life just
caused her tears to flow even harder.
The hangman had done his job quickly and
efficiently and apart from being grey-faced
there wasn't a mark on Roderick other than
the livid weals around his neck. They laid
him gently on the floor of the boat, covered
him with a plaid and once Mary was on board
they shoved off to head down Loch Fyne.

Mary sat staring at her husband's body.
Still holding her baby, she reached forward

and pulled the plaid off her husband's face.
She thought back to how often she had seen
him smile and that never again would he hold
her in her arms. The tears rolled down her
cheeks and she stifled a groan. The wee boy
at her breast awoke and began to grizzle,
sensing that something was amiss. As she
shushed the boy and got ready to give him
the breast, there was a twitch under the plaid.
She looked closer. She hadn't imagined it!
There was a slight movement in Roderick's
left leg.

'Quick lads! I think he's still alive,' she cried.

At once the oarsmen stopped and all turned
to look as she yanked the plaid off the body.
For a third time there was a slight twitch in
his left leg. Then Mary showed that presence
of mind that women seem always able to call on.
Handing the wee child to one of the lads,
she took the little cup that she always carried
on her belt and as quick as she could, pressed
some of her breast milk into it. She then grabbed
the flagon of whisky, pulled out the stopper
and filled the cup to the brim with the amber
nectar. Then cradling her man's head in her
arms she brought the cup to his lips and trickled

some of the mixture between his cold, grey lips.
She had moved so quickly the men in the boat
were in a state of shock. As they looked on,
their mouths hanging open, the liquid trickled
into the chief's mouth and into his throat.
Then came a cough and a jerk and the whole
body convulsed. Mary held on tight as the body
jerked and fell back. Again she trickled the
mixture of breast-milk and whisky between
Roderick's lips. Again there was a jerk and
this time his eyes opened.

'Glory be!' cried Angus Dubh. 'Himself is
still with us.'

At that the chief sat bolt upright and looked
around. He made a strange guttural noise –
a noise which the men in the boat always said
in later years was 'Give me more'. Mary
grabbed him and pulled him close. The lads
began to cheer.

'Wheesht,' said Angus. 'We are still too
close to MacAilean Mor's men.'

Roderick McPhunn looked around him.
He saw his wife, his infant son, his closest friends
and he looked on in amazement at the scene
he found himself in. He was alive. His wife
filled the glass again and pressed it to his lips.

He drank it greedily. By now Mary was crying
tears of utter joy. McPhunn gave a great hacking
cough, shook his head then took her head in
his hands and kissed her, long and deeply as
the crew punched each other in joy.

The cup was filled again and again
and handed round as the chief shook the
hands of the men in the boat, then lovingly
lifted his baby son, looking adoringly at his wife.
Then the McPhunn lads rowed like they had
never rowed in their lives.

Back at Dripp, the rest of the McPhunns
had been getting ready for a funeral. Now they
had something to celebrate and the whisky ran
like water for the next few days. They soon
realised that McPhunn couldn't be hanged
for the same offence twice. He was a free man!
After that they were much more careful and
there are those that will tell you that Roderick
gave up sheep-raiding! What he did not give
up was making and drinking whisky – he owed
his life to the stuff and for the rest of his long
life was always ready to tell the tale of how
his wife had saved his life, with the help of
the *uisge beatha*.

cRafty and canny

EOPLE THROUGHOUT SCOTLAND in
the 18th century made illicit whisky.
The Highlander's attitude that they
had as much right to make whisky
from barley as porridge from oats
was one that found a ready echo in
the Lowlands. In the shadow of the Pentland
hills near the wee village of Carlops, one man
who saw the eminent good sense in this attitude
was one Rollo Scott. He had his still in the
hills above Carlops and if ever he felt there
was a chance the hated gaugers would find
out where he was making his *uisge beatha*
he could simply shut up shop in one enclosed
valley and head off to another. This way he
had for many years avoided being discovered
and the reputation of his whisky grew.
His wares found a ready market in the area
and he even had customers as far away as
Edinburgh, ten miles to the north. All in all
he was pretty successful.

He was often to be seen in the local hostelries
buying drinks and generally having a good time.
While he was supposed to be a farmer everybody

knew damn well that Rollo's ready supply of
cash came from his whisky business and it
galled the gaugers to see him acting like an
upright and well-to-do citizen; but it wasn't
only the gaugers who disliked Rollo. One of
his competitors, a man whose whisky was
never as good as Scott's, increasingly grew
to resent him. Given that he all too often
heard the phrase, 'Aye your whisky is all right
but it's no as good as Rollo's' or some variant
of it, it was little wonder that he had begun
to resent Scott. As he too had his still in the
Pentlands he sometimes ran into his competitor
and had made a point of finding out just exactly
where he had his still.

One day when Rollo was heading into
the hills to start a new batch, he saw a bunch
of gaugers with a pony up ahead of him and
they appeared to be heading to the valley where
he had his still. Hoping that they were just on
one of their general scouting missions through
the hills, Rollo followed them at a distance
making sure he could duck out of sight at any
moment. As they went on his mood grew blacker
and blacker. They were heading directly towards
his still. As they disappeared over the brow of

a wee hill jutting out into the valley his last faint
hopes disappeared. If they were that close
they must have been tipped off. He lay down
in the heather and waited.

Sure enough he soon heard the noise of
his bothie being demolished and a few shouts
of excitement from the Excise men. At last
they had caught up with him. He was furious.
Who could have clyped on him? There were
quite a few candidates. Rollo was aware that
he had offended a few people and he had never
before been bothered by the fact that he had an
enemy or two. But now that it was costing him,
it was different matter entirely.

Soon the gaugers came back over the brow
of the hill leading their pony, with an anker
of whisky and his dismantled still on its back.
Rollo had left that one anker behind on his
last visit and was coming to get it for a
customer over in Carnwath. He would have
to go without now.

The gaugers meanwhile were delighted.
At last they had managed to find and confiscate
Rollo Scott's still. True, they only had the still
and one small barrel of whisky to sell in order
to get some wages, but after having had to put

up with the arrogance of the smuggler so often in the past they were happy to settle for what they had got. They were to take their prize back to Edinburgh. They headed down from the hills and turned north along the ain road to the capital. Soon they were passing through Nine Mile Burn where they had left their cart and given their success they thought it no bad thing if they stopped to toast that success in the inn there.

'Well, well, gentlemen,' said Rob MacLean, the publican as they came through his door. 'You all seem to be in a fine mood today. What can I get you?'

'Well,' said the leader of the gaugers. 'I think we should all have a glass of your very best legal whisky, Mr MacLean. We have plenty of the other stuff already!' He pointed at the door just as one of his men was coming through the door carrying an obviously full anker of whisky on his shoulder. 'And have one yourself, while you're at it,' beamed the happy gauger.

MacLean at once recognised the anker as one of Rollo's – after all hadn't he bought enough of them in the past?

All smiles, he took a bottle of supposedly legal whisky from the shelf behind the bar and poured out six drams, one each for the gaugers and one for himself.

'Here's health to you gentlemen,' he said tossing off his own drama and going through into the kitchen behind the bar-room. Here the three lasses who helped about the place, cooking, cleaning and serving drinks were all gathered. 'Keep an eye on these damned gaugers, lassies and see whit they do with Rollo's anker,' he told them.

The gaugers had another dram and then left. As they tied the anker to the back of their cart beside Rollo's dismantled still, there were at least four pairs of eyes watching their every move through the bar room windows. As the men set off in high spirits, Rob said to the lasses, 'Well if any lass wants a new ribbon, now is her chance if she cuts that string.'

By now the day was drawing on and the gloaming was beginning to settle and if only they had looked behind them, the gaugers would have seen in the fading evening light a young lass come out from the tavern and follow them up the road, keeping well into the shelter of the trees that ran along both sides of the track. This was Helen Barr and close behind her were her two companions from the inn. Waiting till they were a fair way up the road from Nine Mile Burn, Helen took her chance and ran up to the cart. Whipping out a wee, sharp knife she sliced through the hempen cord holding the anker of whisky. As it came loose she grabbed at it with both hands. She need hardly have bothered for her companions had run up and they took the anker from her, placed it down at the side of the road, and run back to the rear of the cart. By now Helen was cutting through the cord holding down the worm of the still. As carefully as she could she lifted it trying to be sure it didn't clatter off the metal body of the still it was resting on. This too was taken by her pals and in a matter of minutes they had successfully removed all of the still from the gaugers' cart. By now they were close to Stoneypath and Rob MacLean had come up on the girls and between the four of them they soon had the whisky and the dismantled still hidden away just a few yards from the road, where no gauger would spot them.

They then headed back to Nine Mile Burn where Rob sent a local lad to find Rollo Scott and let him know what had happened. He was pleased indeed to buy ribbons for the lasses and he and Rob had a fair old drink later the same week in celebration of such dedicated community action in the face of unwarranted government provocation.

As for the gaugers they were furious when they realised they had lost their catch and though they spent most of the following days looking for traces of the still along the road to Nine Mile Burn their efforts were fruitless. As for Rollo, from then on he was even more careful about choosing a safe spot to hide his still and went on to have many more years of great success in his chosen profession.

a Riot in Edinburgh

NE OF THE BEST known families
involved with whisky production
in Scotland are the Haigs. As far
back as 1655 one Robert Haig
was prosecuted in Stirling for the utterly
heinous act of distilling spirits on the Sabbath!
Back then Scotland was under the thumb of
the Presbyterian ministers whose attitude to
joy seems to have been that it should be
considered solely as an attribute of the after-life.
Sabbatarianism of course still exists in parts
of Scotland and it has always struck me that
the need to try to restrict others' freedom to
act in various ways is an attribute of those of
a religious disposition – whatever the particular
religion. As my Auld Uncle Willie used to say,
'I'll leave them be as lang as they leave me be!'
Anyway, the Haigs continued to develop their
distilling skills and were involved from the early
days of the official, government-sanctioned
distilling business.

By the 1780s John Haig had set himself
up in a distillery at Canonmills in Edinburgh.
The capital was beginning to grow and a general,

if limited, increase in wealth was taking place. The prosperous capital was a handy market for the Haig's wares. However, even in the late 18th century, Scotland was a country that feared famine; too many instances of it had scarred the memories of the population and in 1794 again food ran short.

People still talked about the great famine of a hundred years earlier when as many as five per cent of the population are estimated to have died of starvation and so the people of the capital grew nervous. Given the history of the capital over the years, what happened next is not really that surprising. All through the 18th century the Edinburgh Mob had regularly erupted. The Mob had risen in disgust at the corrupt lairdies of the Parliament when they sold out the nation during the Union of 1707; they had stormed again during the Porteous Riots of 1736 and there were regular upsurges of disorder through the capital's streets, many of them led by General Joe Smith. He was a Canongate cobbler who used to rouse the populace by beating a drum along the enclosed streets of Old Edinburgh. Joe had passed away in 1780 but the people of

Edinburgh retained their capacity for taking
to the streets.

No-one knows how or why, but in 1794
a rumour began to circulate through the closes
and vennels of the capital that the Haigs were
using different kinds of grain and even root
vegetables to make their spirits. This was a
foul stain on the reputation of the Haigs who
only ever used barley (with maybe an odd drop
of grain) but the idea that they would make
whisky out of potatoes or turnips and carrots
was plainly daft.

That in mind, rumour is a funny thing
and even the smallest flame can flicker to
a blaze if the conditions are right. And fear
of famine created a gale that fanned this
small flicker to a great roaring conflagration.
Soon people were chattering at close-mouths
and hanging out of tenement windows to pass
the 'news' that the Haigs were buying up all
sorts of foodstuffs for their distillery and thus
forcing the prices up beyond the reach of the
people of Edinburgh.

Given the fear of famine and the long-
established propensity of the Edinburghers
to hit the streets, the riot was almost inevitable.

Starting in Cowgate, a great mass of people headed towards Canonmills, growing at every close-mouth that it passed. By the time they got to the Haig's distillery, the mob was totally out of control and people began to stone the distillery, breaking windows, apparently intent on storming the building and destroying it.

Luckily, for the Haig family anyway, word had preceded the mob and John Haig and his workmen were ready for the rioters. The workforce had had just enough time to get hold of firearms and as the mob attacked they opened fire. Several of the mob fell dead, others wounded, and armed as they were with nothing but sticks and stones they were forced to retreat. At this point the local sheriff or chief law officer, Lord Cockburn, came on the scene escorted by the Town Guard. He proceeded to read the Riot Act which effectively declared martial law and meant that anyone on the streets without what the authorities decided was a good excuse could be arrested and thrown in jail. This was too much for some of the Canongate stalwarts and they headed in a group towards Cockburn's house in George Square. They would show him what they thought of his Riot Act and what they thought of him too! As they headed back up to the town a carriage came towards them

'That's Johnny Haig's carriage,' came a shout. 'Get him.' At once the mob grabbed the horses forcing the carriage to stop and the doors were ripped open. Just as the rioters were about to leap into the carriage, they realised that its sole occupant was a young woman. True enough she was one of the Haigs but they stopped, and let the carriage pass.

On they went towards George Square and at the top of Broughton Street they were met by a couple of local lads who were running to inform them that soldiers of the ninth Regiment East Norfolk were on their way from the Castle. Having already lost a number of their fellows to the firepower of the men at the distillery, the Canongate Boys had no intention of painting the street with any more of their blood, and reluctantly withdrew to leave the streets under the control of the Castle garrison. As quickly as it had flared up the riot died and by the next day all was calm again.

However, John Haig felt it would be a sensible move to put out a public statement and so in the Caledonian Mercury a day later he inserted the following:

'It has unhappily taken possession of the minds of many people that we are using a range of foodstuffs to make our whisky, and that consequently the markets are really affected by the supposed consumption. The genuine truth is that no other species of grain are made use of at Canonmills but barley, rye and sometimes such parcels of wheat as happen to receive damage or are in quality unfit for bread; and that not a grain of oats, pease or a particle of oat-meal, nor any potatoes, carrots turnips or other roots are used in the distillery in any shape, never have been, nor ever will be.'

But such was the paranoia of the powers that be in 1794 that matters couldn't be allowed to rest there. Only two years before some of the Scottish populace had had the utter temerity to hold a meeting of the Friends of the People in Edinburgh and the fear of revolution spreading from France still coursed wildly through the veins of the Scottish establishment. So it was that in early September, two of the rioters who had been arrested and jailed in the Tolbooth were whipped through the streets of Edinburgh;

in a foul echo of the show trials of the Political
Martyrs of the year before, they were transported
to Botany Bay in Australia for 14 years.
It mattered little to Cockburn and his cronies
that the sentence of transportation was one that
had no legal standing under Scots Law.

As for the Haigs, they had done nothing
wrong in the first place and happily their whisky,
made from the finest available malted barley
was soon back in production. It goes to show
that Scots folk do not put whisky before food,
no matter what others may say!

maisie lays down the law

ROUND THE SAME PERIOD as Rollo Scott got his still back, another local entrepreneur had a brush with the gaugers. At the time Carlops, being on the main road from the Borders into Edinburgh, was a thriving place and before the age of the tractor there were a great many more people working on the land. This combined with the thriving cottage industry of hand-loom weaving meant that there was a steady demand for good quality peatreek and Rollo and Johnny Cairns who lived not far away at Steele, were kept busy. In fact Cairns had such demand for his product that he had taken on an assistant, Davie Gray, a handloom weaver from nearby Monks Haugh. But where there was illicit whisky there were gaugers and given that they were ever ready to reward informants and that there are always people ready to grass up their fellows the chance of being raided was always there; the busier the still men got making their drams the less

time they had to pay attention to security.
So it as really just a matter of time before
Cairns was visited by a group of Excise men.

One day Johnny and Davie were heading
up to the still in the Pentland Hills. It was
a damp and sombre morning with banks of
mist drifting through the glens between the hills.
Through the mist they saw a group of men
who they immediately recognised as gaugers.
They were coming from West Linton and the
direction they were heading in made it clear
they had a fair idea of where Cairns's still was;
somebody had given him away.

Luckily they were a fair bit closer to the
still than the gaugers and with the cover of
the mist they managed to get to the whisky
bothie, dismantle the still and bury it in a
nearby bog. They then hid themselves nearby
and watched as the gaugers arrived at the
bothie. Finding nothing, the government men
demolished the crude turf building and headed
back the way they had come. Johnny and Davie
waited till they were well out of sight, before
digging up the still. Now they would have to
find a new location and build a new bothy.
They would lose a day or two's production

but that was a lot better than losing the still itself.

What Johnny didn't know was that while he was hiding from the gaugers on the slopes of Black Hill another group of the Excise's finest had turned up at his home at the Steele. His wife, Maisie had no warning. She was going about her domestic chores when suddenly she found her kitchen full of gaugers.

'Right then lads,' said the leading gauger, totally ignoring Maisie. 'Search the whole place. There is whisky here without any doubt.'

He wasn't wrong. Standing just inside a recess beside the back door into the kitchen stood a small barrel full of Johnny's finest! The bunghole was open and all it would take was one sniff and the gaugers would have it. Maisie though was no fool. Her heart thumping she picked up the funnel she had been using to pour buttermilk from another barrel into a jug. Two of the gaugers were now raking through everything in the room while the other three were either next door or searching through the outhouses. Checking that no one was looking at her, she quickly stuck the filler into the bung hole of the whisky barrel.

The funnel had obvious traces of buttermilk round its lip. One of the gaugers came over and gave it a look. Maisie could hardy breathe and she began to feel a bit dizzy. The gauger was clearly fooled into thinking it was a barrel of milk and went out to join his companions going through the outhouses. They found nothing. By the time they had searched the house and the outhouses and come up empty handed the leading gauger was in a foul mood.

He came to where Maisie was standing at the back door, just a couple of feet from the whisky. 'Well, lady,' he said sarcastically. 'You have got away with it this time, but never fear, our mates have got your husband's still up on Black Hill. We'll see him in court whatever.' He then spat at her feet, turned and motioning the others to follow him, went off back to Carlops.

Once they had gone Maisie had to go and sit down. She had had a dreadful fright. When Johnny got home that night, happy that he had managed to set up a new bothy ready to re-commence production the following day he was met by a white-faced Maisie.

On hearing of what had happened he was

sympathetic and apologised for leaving
the whisky in the house. That was not
good enough for Maisie. She had had such
a shock that she decided to lay down the law.
No more would she allow a barrel of whisky
anywhere near the house, and she demanded
that Johnny give up the business right away.
Try as he might he could not convince her
otherwise and was forced to sell his still.
Luckily, Davie was just the man to take over
and though it meant that he was forced to
go back to working on the land, he did have
access to a steady steam of peatreek made
precisely to the recipe he himself had developed
over the years.

the devil and the highland man

HIGHLAND SCOTSMEN HAVE long been known for travelling the world and a couple of hundred years ago, in the dark years after Culloden, many of them left, never to see their homeland again. Others took to the sea to make a living and spent much of their lives travelling across the world. Towards the end of the 18th century a young lad called Tom Campbell from Wester Ross thought that the sailor's life was for him and joined a ship in Ullapool. His romantic notions of meeting dusky South Sea maidens and sailing along under moonlit skies were soon shattered as he found himself sailing up and down the West Coast and occasionally as far as Ireland.

Now Tom was a tall, broad-shouldered and powerful lad and he had worked for a while in a smithy back home. After only a few months he started to tire of the sailor's life, and began to realise that he had not been too badly off working as a blacksmith. One of the ports that his wee boat called at regularly was Wigtown, and on one trip he was on his way to a dockside tavern for a glass or two of the good stuff when he heard a young lass laughing in the street. Something in the sound intrigued him and he turned to see who was laughing. At that point his life changed.

He saw Jeannie Dixon with a couple of her pals across the street. Jeanie was a wee lass, hardly five foot tall, but what there was of her was all in the right places. She had a lovely, curvaceous figure, long dark hair and a smile that could light up a room. Tom was smitten. He stood there in the street, his mouth agape and stared at the lassie, till his pals dragged him off to the tavern. They only had an hour or two before the ship was due to sail off back up the coast. As they downed their whisky, Tom couldn't get the picture of the beautiful lassie out of his head. So it was that later that evening, as the coaster sailed out of Wigtown, they were a man light. Tom had jumped ship.

Apart from a being a big, handsome lad, Tom had a bit of charm and within a couple of days he had managed to get himself a job with the local smith. That gave him work and a roof over his head and he could now get on with the job of finding and wooing the lass he had spied in the street. It didn't take him long to find out who she was and introduce himself and it didn't take Jeannie long either – to fall for this big, dark, handsome Highland man and soon they were walking out together.

Well, they were young and in love and what happened next is nothing more than the way of the world. Jeannie found herself expecting a baby. Tom had had no intentions whatsoever of settling down in Wigtown when he landed. He had simply been following his heart… well, that and some other inclinations, but he was an honourable lad and soon they were married. They were happy enough. Tom was good provider and after a few years they had three bairns and were living at Glenluce where Tom was working for the local blacksmith. He was a conscientious and pretty skilful worker and fitted right in with the locals, but just as he was a hard worker, he was a hard drinker. Raised since a child to take regular shots of whisky, he thought it no more than his right to have a few whenever he had the mind and the money to do so. Not that he

let Jeannie and the bairns go short; there
was always food on the table in the Campbell
house, but he was known as a man who could
on occasion take a fearsome amount of whisky.

Time passed and one autumn people began
to take ill all over the area. It was a nasty
sickness and soon people were dying in their
dozens. It was as if one of the plagues of old
had come to wreak havoc amongst the folk.
Soon whispers were circulating that it was
all the work of the devil and poor Jeannie
was distraught with fear for her bairns.

'Ach! Dinnae fash, lass,' Tam would say.
'They've aw got my good Highland blood in
them, they'll be aw right, you'll see.' In truth
Tom believed that he couldn't be touched by
this disease. Had not his father and mother
never suffered a day's sickness in their lives?
He had absolute confidence, though occasionally
the worry that Jeanie might fall sick would cross
his mind, but he'd simply brush the thought
away. He could do that; his happy and positive
nature would always shine through.

He decided he would ignore the plague
and carry on as usual. The taverns where he
regularly drank were suffering as so many

THE DEVIL AND THE HIGHLAND MAN

people were sick and others were frightened
of spending time in groups in case they too
could become infected. But Tom was not afraid.
On more than one occasion he was heard to
say, 'Well it might be the Devil's work right
enough, but he'll not get the better of Tom
Campbell.' Then he would toss off his dram
with a hearty laugh. So it was that one night,
he was coming home late from an inn a bit
down the shore of Glenluce Bay with a half
full bottle of the *cratur* in his pocket when
he saw someone on the road before him.
There was a faint moon and he peered through
the darkness to see if he recognised the man.
Man? It was no man. Standing there blocking
his way was the very Devil himself. A bit taller
than Tom, the creature was covered in long
shaggy hair and carrying a great pikestaff that
appeared to be encrusted with blood.

'Campbell, Tom Campbell,' boomed the
Devil in a voice like a bull. 'You have been
laughing at me, now it is time to pay.' He let
out a great roar, intended to make Tom fall to
his knees in terror. He had however misjudged
his man.

'Och, it's you,' said Tom. 'I'd heard you

were abut the place. Will you take drink?' He took the bottle from his pocket and held it out.

The Devil was a bit taken aback at this and instinctively took the bottle. He looked quizzically at the tall Highland man and put the bottle to his lips and took a great slug.

'Och, now, leave a bit for me,' said Tom and swiped the bottle back. At that the Devil looked at him a bit queerly. Now I don't now what kind of booze the Devil was used to but this was a bottle of the real good stuff, all the way from Glenlivet itself and the Great Beast had never tasted anything like it. It was wonderful. Tom had barely had a wee taste for himself when the Devil snatched it from him and poured a goodly portion of its contents down his great hairy neck.

Then the Devil handed the now half empty bottle back to Tom and let out a great hearty laugh. Then he staggered – just a wee bit, but Tom well knew the signs. The Devil was clearly not used to the real stuff. Now that just goes to show that those who say it is the Devil's drink are mistaken for they have nothing as fine as the real stuff in Hell or wherever else the Devil and his minions are hanging out these days. The creature looked at him and a strange look came over his ugly face. Tom realised that the beast was trying to smile!

'Well now,' boomed the great rasping voice, 'you are a Highland man, Campbell are you not?'

'That I am and proud of it,' replied Tom.

'Right then,' the Devil went on, 'I will give you *cothrom na feinne*, the Fair Play of the Fianna.'

By this he meant the ancient honour code of the Highlands that had ruled combat since the dawn of time and always ensured fair play, or was meant to at least.

'And what do you mean exactly by that,' asked Tom.

'We'll wrestle and I'll fight fair, using no magic,' announced the Devil.

'And what are we wrestling for?' asked our hero.

'Why, your soul of course,' laughed the Devil.

'Ah, well then. What if I win?' Tom came back.

At this the Devil laughed again. 'Fat chance, but name your wager.'

'All right then,' said Tom. 'If I win you remove the plague off from all the people, tie it up in a poke and give it to me.'

The devil laughed again and said, 'Done.'

Campbell took a swig from the bottle, noticing a pungent, sulphuric taste from where the Devil's lips had held the neck of the bottle. Sticking the bottle into the pocket of his coat, he set himself.

The pair of them got a grip on each other and started to wrestle. Our Tom had been wrestling since he was a wee boy and was a fit, strong man. Helped by the whisky no doubt, he was sure he could beat the Devil, as long as he fought fair. But he was nearly thrown in the first second. Grabbing the hairy hide of his opponent was one thing but the smell off him was absolutely awful and Tom nearly passed out. Luckily, he held himself together and managed to keep his grip. The pair of them heaved and struggled, staggering across the road and onto the beach. Here, the both of them straining every sinew, they shuffled about till they found themselves up to their knees in the freezing waters of Glenluce Bay with neither managing to throw the other.

'Stop!' cried the Devil as the pair of them began to lose their footing.

They stood back, sloshed out of the water and sat down on some boulders.

'Ach, I just about had you there,' said the Devil. 'Do you give in?'

'What? Me give in?' roared Tom. 'Another couple of seconds and you would have been flat on your back!'

'Nonsense, utter nonsense,' the Devil roared back, but he didn't move to start again. Having agreed to fight fair he was in fact astounded that he couldn't overcome his opponent. As he tried to figure out what to do, he played for time.

'All right, let's call that one a dead heat. Give me another drink.'

Tom whipped the bottle from his coat pocket, amazed that it was still in one piece, and handed it to the Devil, but not before taking a good slug himself.

The Devil tilted the bottle up and took another swig before handing the almost empty receptacle back to Tom who stuck it back in his pocket.

'I know what to do Campbell,' he burst out. 'Can you play the pipes?

'Of course I can play the pipes,' snorted Tom.

'Right then,' the Devil went on. 'Let's have a piping competition.'

'We have no pipes,' objected Tom.

'Aha,' said the Auld Hornie with a leer, 'but we do.'

He snapped his fingers and instantly a set of pipes appeared on the sand.

'I don't know how good they'll be,' the hairy creature said, 'but we'll both have the same advantage, eh? Me first.'

He grabbed the pipes, gave them a blow or two then started to play. Now, as the poet himself has told us, the Devil was a pretty fair piper. He played a set of reels that were foot-stompingly good and people all around Glenluce Bay were woken from their sleep by it. Many were angry but others were impressed by the playing.

When the Devil stopped, he looked at Tom smugly, and said with a laugh, the whisky swirling around in his head, 'Beat that Campbell.'

'Well, I have to say that you are a fair player,' said Tom. 'In fact, I'd say you were better than fair but I suppose I had better have a blow myself.'

He took the pipes and began to play.

And boy did he play. He had never played
so well in all his days. He started with a *pibroch*
that his Uncle William had taught him years
before and soon the Devil's eyes were shining
as he listened to the great sonorous tune ringing
out through the night. Having finished the
pibroch, Tom moved swiftly into a brisk reel
that soon had the Devil's feet tapping.
Then, without a break he moved into a slow air,
an ancient lament that had been handed down
for centuries. The Devil started to cry!
Tears formed and ran down his great hairy
cheeks, he had never heard playing so sad,
so sweet and so tender. Well. Maybe so, but he
had never listened to the pipes after drinking the
really good stuff before, had he? When Tom
finished, the Devil was beside himself with
emotion; never had he felt like this in all his life.

'Tom, Tom! You are a piper my man; a great
piper and I have to say you beat me fair and
square,' he stuttered, his great hairy chest still
heaving with emotion. Then he waved his hands
in the air and a bag appeared in his right hand.
Then he waved his left hand over his head and
a dark, steaming and hissing cloud of what

looked like black mist began to swirl down
from the sky above and as he opened the mouth
of the bag the foul clouds streamed into the bag.
On and on it went till at last there was no more
of it to be seen. Then closing the bag with
his right hand, Auld Nick whipped a long hair
from his nether regions and tied the bag shut
in an instant.

'A bargain is a bargain,' he said, handing
the bag to Tom. 'Here is the plague, but mark
my words Campbell; we will meet again.'
As Tom took the bag the Devil disappeared
in a puff of smoke, cackling an evil laugh.

Tom held the bag, which began to writhe
and jump about. He had beaten the Devil
and got the plague in a bag! He had no idea
what to do next. Who could sort this out?
The only hope was to go and ask the minister,
surely he would know what to do with this
evil bag.

So he ran to the Manse at Glenluce and
hammered on the door. The minister came
and opened the door himself. There he saw
Tom Campbell looking wild and almost mad.

'What is it man? What are you wanting
at this time of night?' he demanded.

Tom blurted out his story holding up the bag which was waving about as if trying to free itself from his grasp. Now the minister could smell the whisky on Tom's breath, but he clearly recognised there was something not right, something demonic, about the bag Tom was holding.

'Stay there till I get dressed,' he barked. 'We'll need help to deal with this.' He turned back into the house. Minutes later he was back fully dressed and said, 'Let's head to the Abbey.'

So in the dark of the night, the pair of them, Tom holding on to the writhing, jumping bag with all his might, headed up to the old Abbey of Glenluce. There they hammered at the great wooden door till a monk appeared. The minister pushed past him demanding to see the abbot himself. The abbot quickly came and all was explained to him. A few minutes later all of the monks of the abbey were lined up in the subterranean crypt, the oldest part of the abbey. They began to chant together. At a sign from the abbot, Tom laid the writhing bag on the altar. All at once a great shrieking sound came up and the monks' chanting grew louder. The shrieking grew louder and the crypt filled

with the sound of a raging wind but the monks
chanted on, louder and louder. The bag went
rigid and seemed to expand. Just as it seemed
it would have to burst, with the chanting roaring
out and echoing from the old stones of the crypt,
there was at last a sharp howl and the bag fell,
apparently lifeless and flat on the altar.
The abbot signalled the monks to carry on and
the chanting went on for several more minutes.
Then with no further signs of life in the bag he
signalled for them to stop.

He picked the bag up and handed it to
Tom. 'Now take this bag back to where you
were given it and leave it there. Have no more
dealing with the Devil and for your soul's sake
forsake the demon drink.'

Tom took the bag, now just like any
other empty sack, and he and the minister left.
The minister walked back with him as far as
the manse, then wished him well. 'Do as the
abbot says; it will be best, and remember
what he said about the whisky, Tom. I will
pray for you.' Patting him gently on the shoulder,
he went into the manse.

Tom was all too aware of the bottle in
his pocket and desperately wanted a wee snifter,

but he restrained himself. First he'd get shot
of this dreadful object, then he'd have a drink.
The abbot and the minister could say what they
liked; he knew that the whisky had given him
the advantage in the struggle with the Devil.
Give it up? Not a chance.

As he came back to the spot where the
wrestling match had taken place he felt a stir
in the bag, and heard the faintest sound of a
muffled laugh. The Devil was mocking him.

'Right!' Tom roared, in a white hot fury.
'I'll sort you myself.'

He laid the bag on a boulder and ran to
the water line and grabbed a great stalk of
seaweed with both hands. Running back to
where the bag was he raised his hands and
brought the hard seaweed stalk down with
a mighty thump. Again and again he battered
the bag, thinking he could hear moaning inside.
He kept on battering the bag till the stalk of
seaweed was split to ribbons. Throwing it aside,
he began to jump on the bag. He carried on
jumping on it till he was streaming with sweat.
The bag was now lifeless; there was no sign of
movement at all.

Just as he stopped to take a breath there

was a loud pop. Standing next to him was the Devil. Still in a great rage, Tom reached out to grab the demon, but he ducked, grabbed the bag and with another pop, disappeared completely. Tom was alone on the shore.

He looked around. All was quiet. Apart from the faint smell of sulphur and marks in the sand there was no sign that anything at all had happened. Tom reached into his pocket and took out the bottle. Slowly, he pulled out the stopper, took a good sniff at the neck and put it to his lips. He always said in later years that that was the sweetest dram he had ever had. He finished the last drops of the nectar, stuck the bottle in his pocket and headed home, exhausted. At home he climbed into bed beside his wee Jeannie and fell asleep, utterly worn out. He slept for about 30 hours – nothing Jeannie could do would wake him.

When at last he did awaken, it was to see Jeanie looking down at him with a wee smile on her pretty face.

'I don't know what you have been up to Tom Campbell, but the minister was here and said I should be thankful for having a man like you,' she said.

'Why, what has happened?' asked Tom

'What has happened? The plague has gone; everybody that was sick woke up well yesterday morning and no one else has died since.'

Tom got up, cuddled his wife and bairns and had his porridge before heading off to work. And did he give up the drink? What do you think? He now had a grand story to tell and it was a measure of the man that he never did see the Devil again. Auld Cloutie had been bested by a good man and a grand whisky and knew better than show his face around Glenluce ever after.

a whisky bet

WHISKY IS POWERFUL STUFF and it is a weel-kennt fact that it can sometimes inspire people, particularly young men, to acts of foolishness. Just such an act of foolishness took place one time at Kirkmaiden in the Rhinns of Galloway. It was the time of the *hairst*, the harvest, and after a long day's graft a bunch of men had gathered in a local hostelry to celebrate the fact that the harvest was in. There would soon be the actual Harvest Home, a festival for all the community to celebrate but this night was a precursor to that. In truth, not all of the harvest was in, but most of it was and the lads were glad the hardest of the work was over and they just in the right mood for a few drams.

As ever a few drams can lead to a few more and as they sat late in the pub the weather, which had been perfectly dry for the previous ten days, began to take a turn for the worse. In fact a storm blew up and as the sky darkened into night a vicious wind was battering driving rain off the tavern windows.

'Aye well,' said Tam Nicolson, a wee bandy-legged man in his early 50s 'We've been lucky lads. Jist about the whole *hairst* is in.'

There were murmurs of agreement, for even though few of the lads there that night were farmers themselves, they were all country men and the need for the harvest to be brought in before the weather changed was ingrained in their very souls, just as it had been in their fathers' and their grandfathers' souls before them.

'Aye. It's a right foul night now,' said Willie McGrew, a shepherd who had come down from the hill to help with the harvest.

True enough, the wind was beginning to blow up into a gale and the assembled company were glad indeed of the whisky they were drinking and more than one or two were putting off heading home because of the weather. As things often did in those days when the weather blew nasty and drink was being taken, the conversation began to drift towards the supernatural. They might have all been regular churchgoers but, as elsewhere in Scotland, the old beliefs had deep roots and could easy come to the surface. Soon there were stories of witches and Auld Hornie, the Devil himself, being told, when one of the company said, 'Well on a night like this I wouldn't pass the old blackthorn at the Maidenkirk for 10,000 pounds.'

This particular twisted old thorn at the gate of the kirkyard at Maidenkirk was less than a couple of miles off and it had long been thought of as bewitched. There were various nods and murmurs of agreement.

'Ach, you're just as bunch o auld weemin,' said young Tom McCulloch, glass in hand. 'What is there to be feart of? I'll tell you what; I'll go and be back in an hour and for proof I'll bring the big kirk bible back wi me.'

'Och, dinnae be daft Tom,' said his pal Andra Mitchell. 'It's a coarse nicht out there and ye'll likely catch yer death o the cold if nothing else.'

But Tom was not to be stopped. Several of the lads tried to get him to sit down as he picked up his jacket and put his cap on his head; he was adamant. He would show them – superstitious old fools, the lot of them – that there was nothing whatsoever to be frightened of. As he was trying to get his jacket on, Andra and a couple of others grabbed his

arms. At that moment a stranger who was sitting
at the back of the tavern spoke.

'Well, lad I'll bet you a golden guinea
that you are not back here in an hour.'
The company all turned to look at him. He was
a tall dark man, dressed in black and in a style
that suggested he was more of a town dweller
than a country man.

'Done,' roared Tom. Pulling himself free
of his friends, he walked over to shake the hand
of the stranger who had got up and come to
meet him in the middle of the room.

Then turning to the rest of the boys he said,
'You all heard that. A bet's a bet. I'll be back
within the hour and I'll have the Bible too.'
Then without another word he pulled on
his jacket and was out of the door in a flash.
Several of the lads looked hard at the stranger
but he just shrugged, smiled and went back to
his seat at the back of the inn. There was a bit
of muttering but more drink was ordered and
nobody thought to go out into the wild weather
to bring Tom back. However, something had
changed; the jollity of the evening was wearing
off and a few of the lads decided it might be
time to get back home. Still, it was a wild night

and it would be a good idea to have a last dram
to counteract the cold.

While the last drinks were being supped,
a horrible noise rang out. It was a great echoing
sound, a sharp and thunderous clanging.
All there knew what that dread sound was.
It was the Wraith Bell that was thought to toll
for the souls of the departed out in the middle
of the bay. The bell had been lost many years
before in a wild storm when all the men moving
it from the old church to the new one were
drowned. Nobody wanted to look at anybody
else. Nobody now wanted to go home. Nobody
knew quite what to do. So they all sat there till
the hour had passed. Then the stranger spoke.
'The lad has not come back, who will come
with me to see what has happened?'

No one moved.

As they all sat there avoiding the stranger's
eyes, he put his head back and laughed.
And what a laugh – it was a wild demonic cackle
that shook the very foundations of the building
and as they all looked on in horror, there was
a great blue flash and the stranger disappeared!
The room was filled with a horrible sulphurous
smell and a whispering voice could just be heard.

'For the love of God, that was the Devil himself.'

Rooted to the spot with fear, the harvesters clung together throughout the rest of that cold, wild night, afraid to set foot outside the tavern in case Auld Cloutie was lying in wait. At last, after what seemed like endless hours, the first light of dawn began to lift the darkness of the night, and the wind began to die down.

As the light of the coming day filled the sky the harvesters came out of the tavern and headed to Maidenkirk. All were terrified of what they would find, but they just had to see what had happened to Young Tom McCulloch. As they neared the church, with the old thorn tree growing by the gate into the kirkyard, they could all see that there was something in the branches. As they got closer, Andra who was in the lead stopped and let out a loud wail, pointing his finger at the thorn tree. There entwined in the branches of the black and twisted tree was the body of Tom McCulloch. The branches of the tree were gripping him like brambles and there in the middle of his chest was a gaping hole where his heart had been ripped out.

On the wall beside the gate lay the great kirk bible and it looked as if the evil spirits sent by the devil had waited till he had placed it down to shut the gate behind him and taken their chance while he was unprotected to work their evil on poor Tom. It was with sad and heavy hearts that his friends cut his body free from that dreadful tree and laid him to rest. Despite the horror if it all no one was ready to cut down the tree and for many long years after it stood there at the kirkyard gate reminding everyone of that evil night. And it had new name after that too – the Man-Wrap.

whisky and sheep

EVEN INTO THE 19th century echoes of the old *cateran* traditions of the Highlands could occur. The old notion that the 'lifting' of livestock was not a form of thieving, but the honourable pursuit of a Highland gentleman (and every Highland male was a gentleman in his own mind) died hard. This was particularly true in some of those clans who had been at the very foremost of the thieving traditions of the Highlands and none more so than the Camerons. Some of them had stayed out after Culloden continuing a sporadic guerrilla campaign against the occupying British Army Redcoats and living off their skills at appropriating livestock. These men were long remembered in popular tales told around the winter fires even as the last vestiges of the old clan society faded away.

And so it was that one day that two Camerons, brothers called William and Lachlan, came to the conclusion that they were as good men as their ancestors had been and decided to prove it. Needless to say, the venture had started off in a shebeen in the west of Lochaber where

they had maybe taken the good stuff a bit
too freely. Our William and Lachlan were,
like so many of their contemporaries, living hand
to mouth, occasionally labouring and sometimes
even having to look after the hated sheep and
the idea that they could return to the ways of
their honoured ancestors and make a fair bit
of cash at the same time was one that was very
attractive indeed. Due to their own shepherding
they had a pair of fine sheep-dogs. Though
drunk when they came up with the plan,
they were not stupid lads. Well, not exactly.

'Now see you here, Lachie;' said William,
the elder by a year and a half, 'if we're going
to do this we will do it right.'

'Of course,' said Lachie, who was as
drunk as his brother and well used to following
his lead.

'Now then, that would mean we will have to
go a fair way away to lift the beasts, you know.'

'Och, I ken that fine Willie,' said his brother.
'Nobody would be daft enough to lift beasts
from next door, now would they?'

'Right, then; we will head off to Fort
Augustus first thing tomorrow and spy out
the land.'

'Ach, why don't we just get off now?' asked
Lachie who had always been a bit impetuous.

'Och, just caw canny, Lachie. Tomorrow's
plenty time and anyway, I have a hankering for
another glass or two here.'

Lachie needed no encouragement to go
along with that.

So the next day the brave lads headed
off towards Fort Augustus. Close to the town
lay the farm of Auchteravon and in a field within
clear sight of the road, a whole herd of sheep
had been gathered together. This was just the
opportunity the lads were after. They vaulted
the roadside dyke and headed to the field of
sheep with their dogs at their heels. Once in
the field it was a matter of only a few minutes
before the dogs had the sheep rounded up and
as Willie held the gate open, Lachie and the
dogs drove the sheep out of the field and
towards the road.

There was absolutely nobody to be seen
and soon the brothers were well on their way
to Fort Augustus. In fact it had all been so
easy that they were absolutely sure that they
had got clean away with the sheep, around
a hundred of them. They would fetch a fair

price in the market at Fort William which
was due to take place the following day.
But as the poet says, 'the best laid plans
of men aft gang agley.'

Willie and Lachie were so confident indeed
that they boldly drove the sheep through the
main street of Fort Augustus, for all the world
just a pair of shepherds driving their sheep
to market. But Fort Augustus, like every
Highland town or village had it fair share
of hostelries, and so, fired up with the ease
of their exploit, the lads decided they should
stop for a dram at a tavern on the north side
of the town. Leaving the sheep under the
watchful eyes of their dogs they stepped into
the tavern and ordered a couple of drams.

A couple of local men were standing by
the rough bar and nodded as they came in.
Then as Willie ordered the drinks one of the
men wandered to the door and looked out
at the sheep. He then came back to his
companion, finished his drink and after
a brief word, left.

As soon as he was out of the door, his
pal turned to Willie and Lachie and said,
'It's a fine day.'

'Aye that it is,' said Willie and raised his glass to the stranger. '*Slainte*.'

'Have you come far?' asked the man.

Lachie looked at Willie who replied to the man, 'Och, not that far at all. We're just heading up to the market with our sheep.'

'That's a fine looking herd you have there,' came the reply. 'You should do well at the market right enough. Can I buy you lads a dram?'

Now this was the kind of offer that neither of the Camerons had ever been known to refuse in their lives and they accepted with pleasure. One thing often leads to another so they bought him one back and soon they were chatting away great guns. Willie and Lachie were having a grand old day to themselves, first they had snatched 100 sheep and now they were making a new friend. However, their companion had a bit more on his mind than making new friends; his pal who had left shortly before had whispered to him as he went, 'That's Andrew McConachie's sheep they have; keep them here while I get word to Andrew.'

Of course the lads had no idea they we being set up and a couple of more drams were taken. By now the light was beginning to fade and night come on. Just as the gloaming was turning to dark, a group of around a dozen men came up the road, all carrying staffs and with grim looks on their faces. Just as they got to the tavern door a couple of young men were coming down the road from the direction of Fort William. These were Davie and Sandy Cameron who were coming to arrange the next delivery of peatreek to the tavern. They had been supplying the place with the illicit spirit for a while now and just happened to be cousins of Lachie and Willie.

As they came into the inn, lit by a single oil lamp at one end of the bar, they could see Willie and Lachie with their backs to the bar surrounded by the group of men with cudgels in their hands. 'Right,' said a tall, red-haired man at the front, 'Steal my sheep would ye, ye filthy swine? Ye're going to pay for that.'

He raised his stick. Willie and Lachie glanced around, terrified. They were cornered; there was no way out. Then Willie saw Sandy through the crowd, but he knew the numbers were too great. If Sandy tried to help them he too would be battered black and blue, at the very least. Just then Davie made his move. He shoved his way to the end of the bar and blew out the lamp. At once there was utter chaos. Willie and Lachie stepped forward into the group of men just as Sandy started shoving into the group from behind. A couple of men tripped over and falling, they sent others sprawling.

'Light the lamp! Dinnae let these thieving bastards get out,' shouted the red-haired man, Andrew McConachie.

By the time the landlord managed to re-light the lamp – having noticed that it was his whisky suppliers that had caused the commotion, he was in no great hurry – all four of the Camerons had managed to get out of the door and hare off into the night.

Willie and Lachie were always grateful to their cousins for saving them from a terrible beating by Andrew McConachie and his friends, probably followed by a spell in jail, and Sandy and Davie never let them forget it. They managed to carry on supplying whisky in the area as no one except the barman had got a good look at them but it was a long, long time indeed before either Willie or Lachie would set foot in Fort Augustus again.

whisky ghost

I T IS ONLY FAIR TO acknowledge that not all the effects of whisky drinking are beneficial. In truth some dreadful things have happened to people over indulging the *cratur* and real tragedies have fallen on some families due to this. As Burns himself told us in 'Tam o Shanter':

> For pleasures are like poppies spread
> You seize the flower its bloom is shed
> or like the snow falls in the river
> A moment white then melts forever...

Sure enough joy can turn to sadness, great fun to tragedy in the blink of an eye. It came about one Saturday on the shores of Loch a Chairn Bhain in the north-west of Scotland. One Saturday morning on the shores of the loch, a local crofter, Donald MacNicol was gathering seaweed for fertiliser when he spotted something just above the tide line a couple of hundred yards away. As he walked towards the object the realised that it was an anker. Generally these wee barrels held two or three gallons of illicit spirit.

He bent down and lifted it. It was actually a bit bigger than the normal anker; Donald reckoned that it must have had more like four gallons in it, and it was indeed full. He quickly checked to see that the bung was tight in its hole. It was! He had no idea how it got here but was more than pleased to go along with the age old idea of 'finder's keepers'. All thoughts of gathering fertiliser for his fields disappeared. This was a fortuitous find and should be celebrated. So he headed straight to Kylesku to find some of his friends to help him celebrate the find by drinking it!

Once at Kylesku he managed to convince the owner of the change house or inn, to let him use the wee upstairs room for a small consideration and set about rounding up some of his friends. Most of them were crofters like himself and among them was his son, also called Donald, who was only just into his 20s. As the men began to climb up the steep and narrow stairs in the change house a local *spae-wife* or wise woman, was passing. This was old Beathag Morrison, a woman who many thought was as almost as old as the hills themselves and who was generally believed to have the gift of second sight, the ability to foretell the future. 'No good will come of this,' she said to the lads going upstairs. 'Mark my words.'

'Ach, we are only having a drink or two;' replied Archie MacLeod, 'leave us alone Beathag.'

They ignored the old woman, set as they were on having a bit of a party. One of the lads brought a fiddle and after a few glasses of the lucky find, they were all singing away merrily. On and on they went. Night came on and they were by then all roaring *fou*, none more so than Young Donald. The night wore on and the elder Donald realised that it was getting close to midnight. After that it would be the Sabbath and though he liked fine to drink the whisky, he was, like most of his friends, a devout man, and would never do anything so sacrilegious as drink whisky on a Sunday. The whole village was strictly Sabbatarian and he shouted above the hubbub.

'Right lads, drink up. It's getting on to midnight and we had better call it a day.' 'Ach dinnae be daft,' shouted his son, slurring his words a little. 'This is a gift from God so He'll no mind us drinking it on his day,' and he started to laugh.

'Enough of that, you,' said his father.
'It's time to stop drinking.'

'Ach, dinnae be so daft faither,' replied
the young man moving to pour himself more
whisky from the jug. His father grabbed him
by the arm to stop him. Young Donald threw
off his father's hand and squared up to him.
The next minute they were trading punches.
Now, Old Donald was well known as a strong
man, but his son had inherited his father's genes
right enough and with the power of youth
he was more than a match for him. He knocked
him across the room, and as he staggered back,
Old Donald tripped and fell headlong down the
steep flight of stairs. They all heard a dreadful
crack and young Donald shouted 'Father!' and
rushed down the stairs. His father lay twisted,
his neck at strange angle and he looked up at
his son, and whispered, 'I shall come back for
my revenge, my lad,' and so saying the light
went from his eyes and there at the foot of the
change house stairs, Donald MacNicol gasped
out his last breath.

Young Donald screamed and ran off into the
night as the rest of the company came down the
stairs to look at their friend's body. Old Beathag

had been right. It was dreadful thing to have happened and Young Donald, wracked with remorse and guilt changed completely. He had always been a happy go lucky lad but now he was gloomy and never smiled. His poor mother almost went mad with grief. People said, as they so often will in cases like this, that the men should have paid attention to what Old Beathag had told them instead of acting like stupid young laddies themselves.

A few weeks later, Young Donald, out fishing in his father's boat fell overboard and drowned; and devout Christians the locals may have been, but no one had any doubt that Donald MacNicol had come back from beyond the grave to have vengeance on his own son. Her son's death finally tipped his mother over the edge and she herself was dead within days. The whisky had brought no-one luck and ever since that day, according to the story, the ghost of Donald MacNicol the Elder has appeared just before midnight on the anniversary of his death. The last reported sighting was in the 1950s, but then we don't know what was being drunk that night, do we?

a last farewell

FUNERALS IN SCOTLAND were generally the cause for a fair amount of the *cratur* to be consumed and it has long been this way. A visitor from south of the border in the 18th century was credited with telling his friends back home that, 'A Scots funeral is merrier than an English wedding.'

Death itself was the root of much superstition and any food in the house at the point of death was believed to be in danger of going off. Thus, a nail or other piece of iron would be inserted into oatmeal, butter, cheese, meat or even whisky to prevent them being contaminated by death. In the case of whisky if this precaution was not taken it was well-known fact that the amber nectar would turn milky white and poisonous, which would be a terrible waste.

As funerals in the old days were essentially public occasions, the communal gatherings to pay one's respects and say farewell to the departed, like weddings, were sometimes held in barns that were emptied and scrupulously cleaned before the event. As at weddings, tables would be set up with food, pipes and tobacco laid out for the mourners. In general the whisky and beer or other potations would be kept under the tables but they would be brought out with such regularity that as things went on they too would end up in plain sight. It was normal for the minister to be invited to this part of the proceedings and to accompany the whole funeral rite. He would generally have a small table to himself and, depending on his own predilections, may or may not have a bottle below it. It was not unusual for a considerable length of time, up to a couple of hours, to pass before everybody thought to be a necessary part of the funeral party would arrive, and this gave the early arrivals a chance to talk about the deceased and how much they were going to be missed as well as to catch up on other news.

Once all were assembled there would be prayers led by the minister, or if he couldn't be there, by an Elder of the local kirk, preferably someone well-known to the deceased. In a country where the church was the focus of much, if not all, social and community activity, this meant there was nearly always someone suitable to fulfil this role. After the prayers, the whisky was rolled out in a serious fashion.

Toddy would be made in bowls for the ladies and those gentlemen who preferred their whisky hot. Many of those who in life had been known for their conviviality made a point of leaving strict orders that their funeral had to be 'weel-plenisht' with whisky. It would be shameful for such a person to go to their death not knowing that their funeral would be a very convivial affair.

Once everyone had a whisky or toddy in hand there would be a toast to the memory of the departed. Bread and cheese would be handed round and then there would be another toast of consolation to the family of the deceased, then another of consolation to the friends of the deceased. Sometimes there would be another toast or two before the final chance to look upon the deceased who all this time would usually be lying in the best room of the house itself. One by one the company would file through the house making their final farewells. While waiting to fulfil this sad task there were of course those who would take another glass or two of the amber nectar.

After the farewells were said, it was time to convey the body to the kirkyard. This was

generally done by the men in shifts of six.
The actual funeral in many parts of Scotland
was restricted to men only, which may just
account for some of the things that transpired.
Sometimes the house of the deceased was
a few miles from the kirkyard and the journey
would not be easy for those carrying the coffin,
even if it was done in shifts.

One such funeral was that of Miss Jessy
Colquhoun on the Braes of Angus. Although
she had never married, she had been a teacher
in the local school and generations of her one-
time pupils came to her funeral. There was
plenty of whisky on hand, for though she was
generally an abstemious woman, Jessy had
taken the odd dram and the chief mourner,
her brother Jamie, a retired army Captain,
had made sure that his sister was going to get
a good send off. It was almost four miles to the
kirk from Jessy's house and as the mourners left,
several of them were carrying bottles of whisky
supplied by Captain Colquhoun. Throughout
Scotland, there are flat topped, roadside stones
known as Lecker Stanes where people would
rest coffins on their way to the departed's last
resting place. There are those that think that

the term Lecker is simply a variant on liquor
for it is a matter of fact that generally when
the coffin was temporarily laid to rest that those
carrying the coffin would take another dram.
There were a couple of these on the way. It was
also very much the custom for the funeral party
to stop at any inn they passed and take another
drink in honour of the departed. And between
Jessy's house and the kirk there were three inns,
even if one of them meant a detour of almost
a hundred yards off the main road. The funeral
party had left Jessy's house just after noon and
it was five minutes past four before they got to
the kirkyard. The Captain, as the primary
mourner was the first to get to the graveside.
There he was met by Auld Tam the gravedigger,
whose patience had been sorely tried waiting
for them all. After all he wouldn't get a drink
himself till Miss Colquhoun was planted in
the ground and decently covered up.

The Captain apologised profusely for
the delay, swaying a bit on his feet as he
did so. 'That's aw very well,' said Auld Tam,
'But whaur's Miss Jessy?'

Colquhoun turned and looked at the funeral
party, which had swollen to near a hundred

strong. All looked at one another. It took a few moments to sink in. Somewhere along the road they had left the coffin! It took a fair bit longer than a moment for the six fittest and youngest of the party to run back to the last inn they had visited and bring Miss Jessy's coffin from its place on the dyke outside the inn to her grave. And in later years it was said that this is when the idea of being late for one's own funeral first arose.

the foondin pint

OW, IT WASN'T INVARIABLY whisky that was drunk at funerals, but it was the preferred tipple. Whisky was taken at all those major social occasions of hatches, matches and dispatches – births, weddings and funerals – but there were other traditional customs that necessitated the consumption of alcohol. One of these was the foondin or founding pint. Whenever masons laid the foundation of a new building there had to be drink taken, usually accompanied by simple food like bread and cheese. Sometimes a little of the drink, but not too much, was poured onto the first stone as a libation and it was believed by all masons that if the ceremony of the foondin pint was ignored, happiness and health would not reign in the house or building being put up. Over time this developed into a regular occurrence and even when building a byre for cattle the foondin pint would make its appearance. After all, the farmer would want his cows to be happy and healthy too.

Back in the early years of the 19th century,

a new manse was being built on the banks of
the Spey. The congregation was thriving and
cash had been raised to give the minister a new
house. The old one had stood since just after
the Reformation and despite the best efforts,
it was a problem keeping the rickety old building
wind and waterproof. So the funds had been
raised for a fine new stone-built manse for the
minister, in keeping with the general and growing
prosperity of the parish.

However, before the first stone was laid
a problem arose. When the foreman asked the
minister about the foondin pint for the building
he was met with a stern reply.

'Strong drink is the enemy of man. The good
book tells us "Be careful, or your hearts will be
weighed down with dissipation, drunkenness and
the anxieties of life, and that day will close on
you unexpectedly like a trap." Luke 21, verse 34.
There will be no drink taken here.'

It was obvious from the minister's words
and the frozen look on his face, that there was
no possibility of the men getting a foondin pint.
It was a cold September day and the masons
and their apprentices had been looking forward
to a bit of a warmer and had hoped for a dram

or maybe even two of whisky. However,
there was no going against the minister;
he was after all paying their wages. So it was
with an ill will and a lot of muttering among
his colleagues that the foreman mason told every
body to get started.

A couple of days later, unknown to the
minister, two of the apprentices visited the
kirkyard just yards away and picked up an old
and broken gravestone that was lying in a corner
on a heap of rubble. They dressed it and included
it in the first floor wall of the manse, just below
the window of the room the minister intended
to use as a study. They had no doubt what would
happen as a result. This would not be a happy
house, it would be subject to odd hauntings and
– it was their fervent wish – the minister would
not last long in his position. And so it proved.
Within a couple of years the minister headed
south having never been able to properly settle
in his brand new manse. As he left, one of the
apprentices, by now a journeyman, said to a
friend, 'That'll teach him tae disrespect the auld
ways. Guid riddance.' As was said later in the
local inn, 'Ye should aye be careful no tae offend
the spirits!' Or should that be spirit?

something similar

SCOTLAND HAS A LONG coastline and it is well known that our people survived the Flood due to the fact that all the west coast people were sailors and had their own boats. Among these hardy souls and their cousins on the East Coast the launching of a new built boat was as important as the raising of a new house. The powers that be had to be propitiated and all possibilities of bad luck avoided. So it was that the tradition among the fisher folk and crofters alike was to break a bottle of whisky over the bows of any new boat once it had been launched for the first time to ensure good luck. After this the whisky and bread and cheese were handed round all present at the launch. The boat would then be named and a blessing spoken over her. This is one such blessing:

'Fae rocks an sands
An barren lauds
An ill men's hands
Keep's free.
Weel oot, weel in,
Wi a guid shot.'

A guid shot here means a fine load of fish.

whisky to the end

COTLAND'S HISTORY IS dramatic and through the centuries there have been many battles; if not against the Romans, Vikings and English trying to conquer us then raids, feuds and squabbles between the various clans have ensured that peace in this land was something greatly to be desired, but not often to be observed. One of the most written about periods of our history is of course the '45; the great uprising that came so close to toppling the Hanoverian monarchy and restoring the ancient House of Stuart. In the years after the great defeat at Culloden on the 16th April 1746, groups of Jacobite Highlanders 'stayed out', defying the Government and living by raiding the Lowlands. While this was an echo of the ancient inter-clan raiding traditions, there were those among them who were perhaps little better than thieves. In this period there was a natural tendency for those who 'stayed out' to link up with the illicit whisky makers of the Highlands who likewise were none too fond of the government and its troops. And Highland warriors were always happier when they had a steady supply of whisky.

Gradually, the Highlands were being pacified and by the time of the late 1750s most of the British Army garrisons had been withdrawn from the Highlands. Strangely enough some of the last areas to be brought under the control of the law were the lands around Inverness.

It was here in 1765 that one of the last of those Highland guerrillas was brought to book. This was John MacMillan who was accused of a whole string of robberies and other crimes. He had been in the Jacobite uprising and ever since Culloden had been living on his wits. The law had at last caught up with him and he knew fine well what his fate would be. His brother had been caught and hanged a few years earlier for a particularly nasty murder that he claimed he had been innocent of. This murder was also laid at John's door but like his brother before him, he denied taking part in it to the very end. On the gallows he denied not just the murder but also claimed that many of the crimes laid at his door were false. However he was a Highlander and he said he knew how to die.

Refusing the offer of prayers from an attending
minister, he told the assembled crowd in
Inverness.

'I wish for no prayers, for myself or for
others. I have a had a good life and have no
fear of meeting my maker. All I would ask
before I go to meet my maker is that I am
allowed one last glass of the *uisge beatha,*
the true spirit of my native land.'

A large glass of whisky was sent for
and delivered to the man on the gallows.
He raised the glass with his bound hands
and shouted, 'Here is a health to Prince Charles
Edward Stewart, the true king of Scots and to
all those who faithfully followed him. I am
a man innocent of the crimes I have been
sentenced for and I call down all the curses
of time on the heads of those who have brough
me here, especially the Sheriff of Inverness who
has been a vicious and cowardly enemy to all
those of the families and followers of Locheil
and Glengarry. Slainte Mor!'

And he tossed off his dram and unflinchingly
stood till the trap door fell open beneath his feet
and he was hanged.